Listening Plu

Authentic recordings with tasks to develop listening skills and learner training

Teacher's Book

Listening Plus

Authentic recordings with tasks to develop listening skills and learner training

Teacher's Book

John McDowell
Christopher Hart

Nelson

Thomas Nelson and Sons Ltd
Nelson House Mayfield Road
Walton-on-Thames Surrey
KT12 5PL UK

51 York Place
Edinburgh
EH1 3JD UK

Thomas Nelson (Hong Kong) Ltd
Toppan Building 10/F
22A Westlands Road
Quarry Bay Hong Kong

First published by Edward Arnold (Publishers) Ltd, 1987

ISBN 0-7131-8451-5

This edition first published by Thomas Nelson and Sons Ltd 1991

ISBN 0-17-556-151-6
NPN 9 8 7 6 5 4 3 2

Cassette produced by David Freeman

Printed in Hong Kong

Contents

Introduction

Listening Plus is a collection of authentic recordings with graded tasks to develop listening skills, integrated with other skills, at intermediate and lower advanced level. It helps learners to improve their general learning skills by encouraging them to think about the learning strategies they use.

About listening

Listening is a complex skill which operates at various levels. It is a skill which involves a series of different strategies and micro-skills that we use at different times for different purposes. These strategies and micro-skills, described below, can be developed systematically to help learners to become better listeners.

- When we listen, we make use of information we already have about the topic being spoken about. The more we know, the less intensively we have to listen. This is because the more information we have, the easier it is to piece together the words and messages we are receiving and to fill in the parts we miss.
- We use the information we already have about the topic, and about how the language works, to anticipate and predict what is coming. All too often, learners approach a listening task with their minds blank when, in fact, they already have highly-developed listening strategies which they use in their own language and which they can easily take over into English.
- We normally listen selectively rather than listening to every word. We listen for key words and expressions that give us clues to meaning, and not to every single word as many learners tend to do.
- As we listen and select information, we store it in short-term memory so that we can reinterpret it in the light of what is to come. We then store it in long-term memory, in the form of messages rather than in actual words.
- We also make use of inference skills to gather information that is not explicitly stated. This includes information about the speakers, their relationship, where they are, what they feel, etc. Our ability to do this depends on our knowledge of the topic and of the language along with its associated cultural conventions.

The material in *Listening Plus* takes account of the complexity of the listening skill and helps learners to develop the different strategies and micro-skills systematically.

About learner training

The main aim of learner training is to help people to become more effective learners. This is a very broad aim, but it is based on specific assumptions about learning:

- all people learn in a highly personal way and different strategies work for different learners, so . . .
- . . . learners should be encouraged to discuss and compare the strategies they are using and to experiment with new ones.
- learners learn what they want to. By having the kind of information the teacher normally has – how the language skills work, how to set objectives, how to use learning material, etc. – they will know better what they want to learn.
- learners often learn more from their peers when they are working independently together than they do from the teacher.
- through knowing more about learning, learners will learn better.

About this book

The specific aims of this book are:

- to help learners improve their understanding of spoken English.
- to train learners to listen communicatively. In doing so, they will

be listening selectively for the message rather than studying the language forms.
• to train learners to listen more effectively. This involves helping them to:
  – use previous knowledge of the topic and of the world in general to predict and anticipate what is coming.
  – listen for key words and expressions.
  – listen selectively for information relevant to each task.
  – use inference skills.
  – develop short term memory capacity.
• to help learners to develop confidence in their ability to deal with and understand authentic spoken English.
• to integrate listening skills with the other skills of reading, writing and speaking.
• to help learners to increase their grasp of linguistic form.
• to help learners to improve their general learning skills by encouraging them to question, assess and develop the learning strategies they use.

About the recorded material

All the recorded material on the tape is authentic in the sense that it has not been specifically written and scripted for language learning, and that it contains a wide range of accents and voice types. Speakers were given general guide-lines to work from but no scripts; the result is a series of spoken texts that have most of the features of normal, conversational English. The quality of the tape is, therefore, not that of a studio-recorded tape as there are background noises and occasional slight distortions. These are due to the natural settings where the recordings were made and so reflect the kind of conditions in which the students will use their listening skills in the real world.
We have chosen the topics and texts that we feel will be within learners' own experience, so that learners can bring their own knowledge of the topic and of the world to help them with their listening skills in a realistic and enjoyable way.

Integrating the material into your course

The material can be organised in your teaching programme in different ways:
• If you are using a core textbook for your course, you can use *Listening Plus* as supplementary material, linking it in through topic areas.
• If you have no basic core book, you can use *Listening Plus* as a resource book and link it to other materials through topic areas, skill development, or project work.
• The material can also be used by learners working on their own.

Using the material

Each unit is organised in a slightly different way and a variety of exercises and task types is offered in each one. This teacher's book gives you detailed teaching notes on how to exploit the material, but here are some general points to keep in mind:
• You should work through Unit 0 before doing any of the other units. It gives learners essential information about the listening process and shows them some of the listening strategies they can use with the rest of the material. Once you have done this, there is no need to work through the other units in the order in which they appear in the book nor to do all the work in any one unit.
• The material is designed to *develop* listening skills, not to test them. The tasks therefore move from global understanding, to more detailed understanding of the message, and then on to attention to some of the linguistic forms. This development is important, as it ensures that the learner is led to understanding through a series of graded steps and is freed from the feeling of having to understand every single word.
• The language is not graded, but the tasks are.
• The listening skill is integrated with other skills. We feel that this is an important part of the approach that adds to the quality of learning. We also feel

that it is important that the activities are carried out in the different modes indicated – individual, in pairs, in groups, or whole class.

• Learner training is an important dimension of the material. By performing different tasks, and through the topics of some of the units, the learners are encouraged to think about and discuss their attitudes to learning and the strategies they use. They should be allowed to talk freely about this and be encouraged to form their own conclusions. There are no right or wrong ways to learn; there is only what works for each individual.

Unit 0 Handy Hints

The objective of this unit is to help learners to use *Listening Plus*. We, the authors, believe that an important aspect of learning a language is learning and knowing how to learn. This unit offers material to make learners more aware of how we listen, and gives learners some hints on how to listen more effectively.

Objectives

1 To develop listening skills of:
- listening for specific information.
- listening for gist.
- interpretation and inference.
- listening with anticipation.

2 To develop the reading skill of:
- reading for specific information.

3 To develop speaking skills through:
- discussion.

4 To develop learner training through:
- discussion and comparison of difficulties in listening.
- analysis of the listening process.
- exemplification and practice of listening strategies.

The title

This unit is called Unit 0 because it is an introduction to *Listening Plus*. In British English the figure 0 is called 'nought', while in American English it is often called 'zero'. 'Handy hints' are little pieces of useful, practical advice.

Task 1
Warm up: reading and speaking

Tell the learners to work in pairs or small groups and ask them to think about the things that cause them problems when they are listening to English. Tell them to read in their books the comments made by English learners of other languages, as these will almost certainly make them think of a lot more points. Encourage them to discuss their ideas together and to make a list. Finally, tell them to keep their lists until the end of the class, when they will be able to see whether this unit has given them any ideas on how to deal with their problems.

Task 2
Reading

Tell the learners to read task 2 in their books, which points out some features of the material in *Listening Plus* and explains some aspects of the listening process. Encourage them to help each other with any comprehension difficulties and to discuss the content of the text if they want to.

Task 3
Listening

3a Tell the learners that they are going to practise listening for key words. Explain that, even for a native speaker, it is not immediately clear what the two people they will hear on the tape, Ruth and Nigel, are talking about. Explain that they are going to do the same as a native speaker – listen for clues.

Play the tape and tell the learners to listen for the key word that is repeated various times. Allow them to discuss their answers, and play the tape again as many times as they feel necessary. Then check their answers and ask them to make a guess about what the conversation is about.

Key

The key word is 'play'.

Tapescript

Ruth: Oh I'll play in that, if I'm here. Yeah.
Nigel: Yeah. You played last year as well, didn't you?
Ruth: (When is it?) Yeah, I played last year. Did you?
Nigel: (Yeah. It's at the end of this month.) No, I played at the one earlier this summer.
Ruth: Mm, but you didn't play last year?
Nigel: Not last year, no. I gave them a rest last year.
Ruth: Thought you'd stun them this year.
Nigel: Which I did do.

3b Now tell the learners that they are going to hear the rest of the conversation which makes it clear what the topic of conversation is. Tell them to listen and to make a note of all the words that give them clues. Play the tape as many times as the learners feel necessary and allow them to discuss their answers after each playing. Finally, elicit their answers and check them with the tape.

Encourage learners to follow this same strategy whenever they are using the listening material in this book. Point out that, although they did not understand all the words on the tape, they were able to work out what Nigel and Ruth's conversation was about by focusing on the key words. Ask them to read the paragraph in their books which points this out to them.

Key

The topic of conversation is 'playing tennis'. The words that give clues are:

tennis play set five two won

Tapescript

Ruth: Which you obv.. well you obviously have if you get invited by the chairman. Wow. Things are moving up, aren't they?
Nigel: This is true. This is true. Do you enjoy tennis then?
Ruth: Yes and no; I don't play regularly enough to be any good so I get very frustrated. But um, no, I didn't have any friends who played in London last year, um, because my good friend who lives round the corner, she doesn't play, but this year someone else's moved in the area and plays a lot so, um, I've started playing with her now.
Nigel: A sort of regular event.
Ruth: Well, trying.
Nigel: Who normally wins?
Ruth: Um, it's very even at the moment. I think we're two matches all. It's a bit tense.

Nigel: . . . . .
Ruth: Last night was very tense. She won the first set, so and then she was five two up in the second so it was a bit of a fight, but I won, I won.

Task 4
Listening

This is a more difficult example of the same type of strategy, but, this time, the learners will also have visual clues to help them.

Tell the learners that they are going to hear Alison talking at a dinner party and that they will have to guess what she is talking about. Explain that you will play the tape as many times as they find necessary and that you will gradually give them clues to help them.

Play the tape and tell the learners to try to guess the topic of conversation and to note down the words that helped them. Warn them that this is the most difficult stage and tell them not to worry if they catch very little. Play the tape as many times as they feel necessary and allow them to discuss their answers after each playing. Finally, elicit their answers and write them on the board. Do not comment on them or correct them at this stage as they are going to get more clues to help them.

Now tell the learners to look at the pictures on the next page in their books and to guess which one matches what Alison is talking about. Allow them to discuss their answers together, and play the tape again if they feel it necessary, but do not give them the correct answer yet. By now all the learners should be feeling more confident about the task.

Tell the learners to read the questions a–d under the pictures in their books, and the list of words they should use in their answers, and make sure that they understand them. Play the tape again as many times as the learners feel necessary and allow them to compare answers after each playing. Finally, check their answers.

Now ask the learners to read the paragraph below the questions in their books, and discuss it with them if necessary.

Key

Picture 2 corresponds to what Alison is saying.

a The experience Alison describes occurred when she was about 13.
b Because her teeth protruded and were crooked.
c Metal rings were put round each tooth and a wire linking all the teeth together. Top and bottom teeth were joined with elastic bands.
d For three and a half years.

Tapescript

Alison: When I was about 13 they said, 'You're going to have a brace', and I thought 'Oh yeah, you know, a simple little band round my teeth' (Yeah.), and they showed me this picture and I had to have it top and bottom, and every (Gosh.) tooth was ringed round with metal (I know, yeah.) and a metal tab put on the front, and then a wire linking all the teeth together. (I don't think that they need to do that, because my tee. . I mean my teeth stuck out like that 'cos I sucked that finger, and all I had was a metal band, one thin band across.) But mine were sort of like a zig-zag along the bottom and (A real mess, weren't they?) (Ah, I see.) and the eye teeth were (Yeah, I had hoops on my eye teeth.) sort of er (They're very good now, aren't they?) ninety degrees, ninety degrees round. (Oh I see.) And then I had elastic bands linking my top teeth to the bottom teeth (Ugh.) (Oh my God.), 'cos my jaws were in the wrong order; and I had this on from thirteen . . they said it was going to be on for a year and it was on for three and a half (other voices); and I didn't speak for about . . . 'cos I wasn't supposed to eat between meals, and I hardly spoke for about three years 'cos it was such an effort with these elastic bands which used to pin my mouth back.

Task 5
Listening

This is a much more difficult task to demonstrate the same point. In order to show that we normally listen for key words rather than trying to catch every single word, we have taken the weather forecast from the radio and erased from the tape all but the essential words. This may make the task very difficult for some learners. Warn them of this before you start so that they do not become discouraged.

First tell the learners to look at the map in their books and to say where they would expect to find it and what they would expect to hear on the tape which accompanied it. This will make the listening task easier as they will know the kind of language and information to expect. Stress to learners that when they listen to anything, they themselves may often hold a lot of information which could help them with their listening.

Tell the learners to look at the questions in their books, and then play the tape. Allow them to compare their answers, and play the tape again as many times as they feel necessary, allowing them to compare answers after each playing. Then elicit their answers and check them with the tape.

Ask the learners if they would like to comment on the implications of this task. However, do not force them to speak. Point out the fact that they were able to understand and answer the questions even though they did not hear the complete text. This seems to suggest that understanding depends on hearing the key words rather than on catching every single word. Ask them to read the paragraphs below questions a–c in their books. Discuss anything the learners wish to.

Key

a There are thundery showers.
b It will be dry (no rain) and humid. The temperature will be 12°C.
c It will be misty.

Tapescript

The local weather . . . . thundery showers . . . . die out . . . . night . . . . dry . . . . Humid night . . . . temperatures . . . . .

. . . . 12° . . . . Misty . . . . dawn.

Task 6
Listening

This is a slightly different kind of exercise, and is used to demonstrate that it is often possible to hear only one side of a conversation and to guess what the other person taking part is saying.

Tell the learners that they are going to hear Tina, who was at the same dinner party as Alison, phoning a friend. Explain that they must listen straight through the tape once, and then must listen again and write down what they think the person at the other end of the line is saying.

Play the tape straight through once, and then as many times as the learners feel necessary. Allow them to discuss their answers after each playing. Finally, elicit their answers and write them on the blackboard. There is no one right answer, so write all the appropriate answers.

Key

(As there is no one right answer, this is only one possibility.)

. . . .

Friend: Yes, just a moment.

. . . .

Yes.

. . . .

Yes. Fine.

. . . .

Well, I was in bed.

. . . .

Great. What time will you come round?

. . . .

Oh yes. I'll be ready.

. . . .

Sorry?

. . . .

Yes. I promise I'll be ready.

. . . .

Where are you phoning from?

. . . .

Where?

. . . .

Stockwell?

. . . .

See you. Bye

. . . .

Tapescript

Tina: Hello, is Jackie there please?

. . . .

Thanks . . . . Hello, Jacks?

. . . .

Hi. It's Tina. Alright?

. . . .

Good. You sound really tired.

. . . .

Oh. Oh sorry. Yeah. Obviously we're going to be late home. So, erm, what we'll do, we'll pick you up tomorrow.

. . . .

About, what time? (Other voice in room: a quarter to twelve) About a quarter to twelve. Is that OK? Make sure you're ready.

. . . .

You will, promise?

. . . .

Promise you'll be ready on time?

. . . .

OK then.

. . . .

Oh, we're at a friend's of Alison's. We've just had a meal.

. . . .

Oh Sss . . . Where are we? (voice in room: Stockwell) Stockwell.

. . . .

Yeah. We've just had a really nice meal. Yeah. So. OK then, OK then.

. . . .

See you then. Right. Bye.

Task 7
Listening

This task is similar to the previous one and should be handled in the same way.

Key

. . . .

Speaking.

. . . .

Yes. They got here this morning.

. . . .

You didn't give me your credit card number.

. . . .

Yes, please.

. . . .

Yes, I think so. But phone me before you come, please.

. . . .

Goodbye.

Tapescript

John: Hello, could I speak to Mack, please?

. . . .

Ah, this is er John McDowell. I was just phoning to make sure you'd got my cheques this morning.

. . . .

Yes? Ah good.

. . . .

Oh, didn't I? Do you . . . shall I give it to you now?

. . . .

Just a moment, please . . . . Hello. Sorry, I didn't realise I had to do that. Um, it's 4929 764 465 122. That's a Barclaycard Visa. Um, do you think . . . you'll have the ticket by tomorrow if I pop up, or . . .

. . . .

Yeah, I'll give you a ring before I come up so . . . just to make sure. Oh. Thank you very much. Bye bye.

Task 8
Extension activity

Ask the learners to look back at the list of difficulties which they compiled in task 1. Ask them to talk about whether they have now found any ways of solving some of them.

Unit 1 Storeys From Spain

This unit deals with descriptions of buildings. The listening activities are based on descriptions of a square in Vic, a town in Catalonia in the north-east of Spain.

Objectives

1 To develop the listening skill of:
  – listening for specific information.
2 To develop speaking skills through:
  – information gap activities.
3 To focus on the following language points:
  – adverbs of degree (*very, particularly*, etc.).
  – the vocabulary for naming parts of a building.
  – language to express uncertainty or tentativeness, such as *it seems, it looks as though, sort of, Dutch-looking*.

The title

The title is a play on the words 'story' (plural: stories) and 'storey' (plural: storeys). One of the main features of the buildings described on the tape is the number of storeys they have.

Task 1
Warm up and language focus

The purpose of this task is to prepare the learners for some of the vocabulary which they will hear on the tape and will need to use during the unit.

1a Tell the learners to look at the drawing in their books and to use the words beside it to label the different parts of the buildings. Encourage them to work in pairs and to help each other.

Key

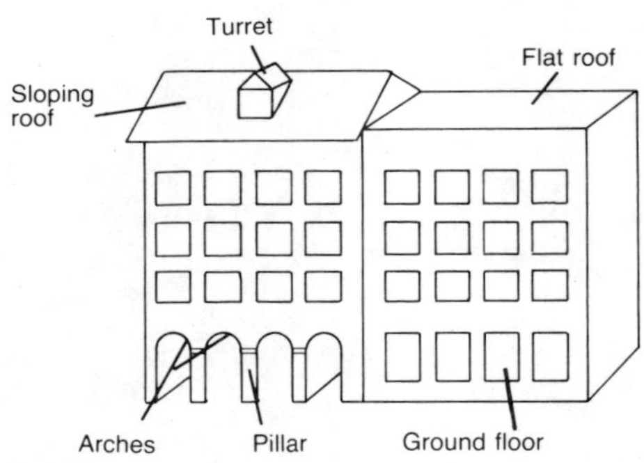

1b Tell the learners to make a list of all the other words they would need to describe the buildings. Elicit the words they have noted down and write them on the blackboard.

Task 2
Listening

Tell the learners to look at the photograph in their books, and explain that it is the main square in Vic, a small town in Catalonia in the north-east of Spain. Explain that they are going to hear six people describing different buildings and that they will have to decide which building each person is describing. Point out that some of the people describe the same building.

Depending on the level of your class, either pause the tape after each speaker and allow the learners to discuss their answers, or play it straight through and allow them to compare answers at the end. In either case, play the tape as many times as the learners feel necessary. Finally, elicit their answers and check them with the tape.

Key

1 *Peter*: building 2.
2 *Alison*: building 5.
3 *Nigel*: building 3.
4 *Brenda*: building 5.
5 *Elizabeth*: building 3.
6 *Deborah*: building 9.

Tapescript

1

Peter: Ah yes, the building, erm, is . . . it's a three storey, four storey building, erm, with a small turret on top of the roof. Erm, it's, t'has three windows on each floor, and each window has a balcony. Erm, it's stucco, stucco-fronted, erm – looks as though it might be a hotel, maybe of some sort.

2

Alison: The building I like is this one at the bottom of the square, in the middle; I think it probably one of the oldest buildings in the square and I . . it seems to be the Town Hall. It's got two very nice, very graceful, curved arches on the ground floor, and then it goes up about three floors with tall, narrow windows and a balcony which is rather nice which I suppose looks over the square, and a flag hanging down from it. And then at the top there's a, there's a set of small, very graceful carved stone or plaster pillars.

3

Nigel: This is a particularly ugly-looking building. About four storeys high. It's got two balconies, about eight windows, two of which are shut. At the bottom you can't see anything 'cause there's total darkness there. It seems to have a sloping roof, and a drain pipe running down one side.

4

Brenda: This building is in the centre of a long row of buildings. It has two arches at the base on the ground floor. And it looks like it's got a banner hanging from the second floor, which has got writing on it which makes me think it's probably displaying some information about an exhibition or something that's on, so I think it's probably a museum or an art gallery. Er, it has four storeys altogether and something that might be another storey at the very top with lots of little windows across, and a small balcony across the roof.

5

Elizabeth: It's it's a very narrow building, part of a terrace of similar buildings but they're all different heights and this one is narrower and lower than the others. It's five storeys, and the bottom floor is made up of a kind of, er, shopping arcade; and then there's two windows on each floor above that, erm, two of which have quite attractive little wrought iron balconies; and er, then it has a sloping tiled roof at the top, and it seems to be sort of squashed in between the other buildings, erm – just possibly added later.

6

Deborah: This is a building which is pretty big, and it looks like a variety of architectural styles but it's quite difficult to tell which ones they are. It's got a kind of open . . I think it's an open gallery under a roof at the top – probably is a gallery; and I don't think the window, I don't think there are any windows, I think it is actually open to the air; and a little gable which looks sort of Dutch-17th-century influence which is rather nice. And on the corner, it's got a huge, very-difficult-to-describe kind of structure, which is made up of little pillars, and little cornices and another Dutch-looking little building on the top. And I suppose it might be a bell tower, or might have been a bell tower, at one time. And you can probably get up right to the top.

Task 3
Language focus and listening

The objective of this task is to focus on expressions which convey uncertainty or tentativeness using the verbs 'seem' or 'look'. Write on the blackboard the two examples given in the student's book and make sure the learners understand the meaning of them. Then tell them to listen to the tape again and to note down all the expressions they hear that contain 'seem' or 'look'. You can either play the tape straight through or tell the learners to ask you to stop the tape every time they hear an expression. Tell them to try to write down one expression for each speaker. Then ask them how the expressions differ.

Key

1 *Peter*: 'it looks as though it might be a hotel'.
2 *Alison*: 'it seems to be the Town Hall'.
3 *Nigel*: 'it seems to have a sloping roof'.
4 *Brenda*: 'it looks like it's got a banner . . .'
5 *Elizabeth*: 'it seems to be sort of squashed in'.
6 *Deborah*: 'it looks like a variety of architectural styles'. '. . . which looks sort of Dutch 17th century . . .'

Task 4
Speaking

This is an information gap activity based on task 2. The objective is to allow learners to use for themselves the language which they have been listening to in this unit. Tell the learners to work in pairs or small groups. Ask them to take it in turns to describe a building in the photograph of Vic while the rest of the group tries to guess which building they are describing.

Task 5
Language focus and listening

This is an activity to focus on adverbs of degree. Write the following example on the blackboard: '*very* ugly'. Tell the learners that they are going to listen to the tape again and that they must write down all the other adverbs of degree that they hear.

Key
Alison: very, rather.
Nigel: particularly.
Elizabeth: very, quite.
Deborah: pretty, quite, rather.

Task 6
Language focus and listening

This task draws the learners' attention to the different ways in which Deborah describes features of the building which she cannot be exact about.

Write on the blackboard the four different expressions given in the student's book and play the tape again (only the last section, when Deborah speaks) so that the learners can check that they understand the expressions and how they are used.

Task 7
Speaking

The purpose of this activity is to give the learners a chance to use the language which they looked at in task 6.

Arrange the learners into pairs or small groups and tell them to describe the photograph in their books, making use of the language they have studied in the unit.

Extension activity

Collect a set of unusual photographs or drawings similar to the one used in task 7. You will need at least enough for half the class to have one each.

Arrange the learners into pairs and give each pair a drawing. Tell them to write a description of their drawing and to be careful not to show it to any of the other learners in the class. When they have finished, collect all the descriptions and drawings. Separate the drawings from the descriptions and display them on the wall or on tables, with the drawings together on one side and descriptions on another. Then tell the learners to try to match the descriptions with the drawings.

Unit 2 Phobias

This unit is about phobias and fears. Most people experience phobias or irrational fears at some time in their lives. They are very personal feelings and some people do not like to talk about them. It is important not to embarrass learners by forcing them to talk about their own fears if they do not want to.

The topic was chosen because it is interesting and usually provokes animated conversation and discussion – perhaps because we all love talking about ourselves.

Objectives

1 To develop listening skills of:
- listening for specific information.
- interpretation and inference.
- listening with anticipation.
- intensive listening.

2 To develop reading skills of:
- reading for specific information.
- reading for pleasure.

3 To develop speaking skills through:
- personalisation tasks.
- discussion.

4 To develop learning skills through:
- becoming aware of aspects of the listening skill that cause difficulty, in order to know what to concentrate on.

5 To focus on the following language point:
- verbs and expressions which refer to being afraid.

The title

Phobias are irrational fears: for example, someone who is terrified of being in a place where there are spiders suffers from a phobia.

Task 1
Warm up and language focus

The expressions in the box in task 1 are used on the tape to describe fears and anxieties, and it is important that learners understand their nuances of meaning before beginning the listening task. Encourage the learners to work in pairs and allow them to use a dictionary, preferably a monolingual one.

Key

strong	**quite strong**	**not so strong**
phobia	anxiety	uneasiness
terrified of	afraid of	makes me feel uneasy
petrified of	can't stand	
	hate	

Task 2
Listening

Tell the learners that they are going to hear five people talking about things that frighten them, and explain that they are real people talking about their real fears. Tell them to listen and to write down what each person is afraid of.

Depending on the level of your class, you could either pause the tape after each extract and allow learners to note down and compare their answers, or you could play it straight through without stopping and allow learners to compare answers at the end. In either case, play the tape as many times as the learners feel necessary. Then elicit the answers from them and check them with the tape.

Key

Donald: rats; being eaten by rats.
Pat: dogs; being attacked by dogs.
Tina: being trapped in a car and burnt to death.
Mike: putting his head under still water, e.g. in swimming pools. (He is happy to swim in the sea.)
Deborah: flying in an aeroplane that someone else is piloting.

Tapescript

1

Donald: I've had a similar experience . . . in in Africa . . . and, er, was living in a house . . . and . . . I knew there were rats about because I could hear them at night . . . scratching . . . and . . . then I found that they had got into the desk and . . . er . . . and there was, there were rat droppings in my . . . in amongst all my papers, in the drawers, and they had also got into my suitcase. There were rat droppings in amongst my clothes in my suitcase. And then one night I could hear them in my bedroom, and they were scratching and scampering around on the floor, and I was absolutely petrified . . . I didn't dare get out of bed because I thought, 'As soon as I put my foot down on the floor one's going to come up and start eating me . . . or at least start biting my toes.'

2

Pat: I really can't stand dogs. I hate dogs more than anything else in the whole world. Erm, I don't like them. I don't trust them, I feel that they're . . . no matter what anybody says . . . how tame they say they are or domesticated they are . . . I think that innately that they are, erm, hunting animals and I just feel that they're not to be trusted; and I think that my . . . distrust and dislike of them is compounded by the fact that I was actually attacked by a dog when I was really little when I was four and I just won't . . . I wouldn't forget it . . . and I just can't trust dogs.

3

Tina: I've got a fear of being blown up in a car. I think it's probably because, when I'm in a car, especially if I'm in the back, I feel quite claustrophobic. And also to me being burnt . . . dying of being burnt . . . is a really horrific . . . way of dying I think, and . . . when I'm in a car sometimes if I can smell petrol I get very very panicky, and I always think I'm going to blow . . . you know, blow up in the car.

4

Mike: Erm, it's very hard to understand why I don't swim and I think it has to be put down as irrational fear of water . . . not so much water in itself, but of losing control . . . of putting my head under water. Erm, I'm quite happy to have my body in water, I don't mind waves breaking over my head as long as there's some spaces for air within that water. What I don't like, and what I lack the strength of will to do, is to consciously put my head under a flat surface of water. Erm, I think it's something to do with swimming pools as well. They . . . the white tile and the smell of chlorine, they've always reminded me of flooded mortuaries, I must admit. Erm, I find I'm much happier in the sea where the surface is choppier, rather more broken.

5

Deborah: Yes, I've been on two trips to Switzerland by plane, er, a few years ago now when I was fifteen and sixteen, and I was terrified, and – both times – and even more terrified the second time than the first. I don't like the idea of being in a small enclosed space with somebody else in control. . . . I've worked out that . . . and with nothing else beneath me . . . I've worked out that if I was flying the plane I'd feel very happy, but I don't like someone else doing it for me.

Task 3
Discussion

Tell learners to work in pairs or small groups and ask them to make a list of all the fears and phobias that they can think of. There is a surprising number of them and some of them have special names.

agoraphobia – a fear of wide open spaces
claustrophobia – a fear of small, enclosed spaces
vertigo – a fear of heights
hydrophobia – a fear of water
phobaphobia – a fear of developing a phobia!

This is an opportunity for learners to share anecdotes or to talk about their own fears. This should develop naturally: learners should not be forced to talk about themselves if they do not want to.

Task 4
Listening

Explain to the learners that they are going to hear a psychiatrist defining the term 'phobia' and that they will have to compare his definition with the one given in the extract from the dictionary in their books. Explain that they will then have to analyse the five cases from task 2 according to these definitions.

4a Tell the learners to read the dictionary definition, then play the tape and let them compare their answers with a partner. Play the tape again as many times as the learners feel necessary and allow them to discuss their answers after each playing. Finally, elicit their answers and check them with the tape.

Key
Dr Hart defines a phobia as a fear 'completely out of proportion to the danger posed'; that is, as a fear which is quite irrational.

The dictionary points to three factors:
– the fear must be irrational.
– there is a compelling need to flee from or avoid the object of fear.
– the fear must be persistent and intense.

Tapescript

Dr John Hart: Um, it's quite normal to be afraid of something which is dangerous. The interesting thing about phobias is the panic or the anxiety which it creates is completely out of proportion to the danger posed by that particular object. Erm, for instance, the rats carry disease and do bite so it's fairly sensible to be afraid of rats. But if the rat's not in a position to attack you or bite you and you are absolutely terrified by its presence, then that's out of proportion . . . and that is phobic.

4b Now tell the learners to work in pairs or small groups and to decide which of the people they listened to in task 2 may not have a phobia. Play the tape for task 2 again if the learners feel it necessary.

Key

Donald's fear of rats may be perfectly reasonable. They are dangerous animals, especially in large numbers or when trapped. They also carry diseases such as rabies.

Task 5
Listening

Tell the learners that they are going to listen to Dr Hart defining three types of phobia. Explain that they will have to note down what these types of phobia are and then classify the cases of the five people from task 2 according to type. Play the tape as many times as the learners feel necessary and allow them to discuss their answers after each playing. Finally, elicit their answers and check them with the tape.

Key

a The three types of phobia are:
1 fear of objects, e.g. spiders and rats.
2 fear of social situations, e.g. speaking to groups of people; being in crowded lifts.
3 fear of objects with which the person has had a bad experience in the past.

b *Type 1*: Donald. Possibly Tina, Mike and Deborah.
Type 2: Possibly Tina, Mike and Deborah, though their cases could be classified as type 1.
Type 3: Pat. (Tina and Mike have specific fears that may have been provoked by an initial bad experience. However, there is no evidence on the tape to support this.)

Tapescript

Dr John Hart: No one knows really why, um, people develop phobic syndromes. There are several kinds of phobias. Erm, there are objects which people are commonly afraid of, as you mention, like spiders, rats, erm, er, other, erm, dangerous objects. There are people who develop phobic reactions about social situations, erm . . . perhaps talking at cocktail parties, or being in crowded lifts, or being on their own in wide open spaces. Erm, people develop phobic reactions towards objects that they've had a bad experience with. Commonly, children who have been bitten by a dog may never settle down and feel comfortable with dogs, but always feel this, er, tremendous anxiety when they're nearby. So there are those patients or those people to whom one can see what seems to be a cause, and those in whom one never ever finds an initial . . . bad . . . er, situation.

Task 6
Listening

Tell the learners that they are going to hear Dr Hart talking about 'free-floating anxiety' and that they will have to listen and answer the questions in their books. Let the learners first read the questions, then play the tape as many times as they feel necessary, allowing them to discuss their answers after each playing.

Key

a According to Dr Hart, 'free-floating anxiety' is a general feeling of anxiety or discomfort in everyday life.
b People do not tolerate it: they find an object on which to fix it.
c All of them except Pat.

Tapescript

Dr John Hart: With anxiety . . . about fairly innocuous harmless things like spiders and insects, usually it's difficult to pinpoint an unpleasant occurrence involving these objects in childhood. Erm, and so one has to look for other reasons why the anxiety is particularly attached. Normally, erm, if one looks very carefully at the person and their past experiences, one will find a totally unrelated emotional disturbance, which, until the onset of the phobia, is characterised by free-floating anxiety or a general level of discomfort in everyday life. Now, human beings don't tolerate free-floating anxiety particularly easily, and it's much easier to the, er, psychological self to attach that to a specific object. Characteristically, people who are unhappy in their family life, instead of being distressed all day long to the extent which they couldn't cope at work or they found their general existence very uncomfortable, may seize on a particular issue which becomes the . . . kind of . . . er, centre of their anxiety if you like, and allows them to lead a normal life the rest of the time.

Task 7
Listening

Tell the learners that they are going to hear Dr Hart describing one form of treatment for people with a phobia and that they will have to make notes on it, and will then have to apply the method to one of the five cases from task 2.

7a Tell the learners to listen to the tape and to make a note of the different stages of treatment for someone who is afraid of spiders. Play the tape as many times as the learners feel necessary and allow them to discuss their answers after each playing. Finally, elicit their answers and check them with the tape.

Key

1 Sit the patient in a large room.
2 Put a picture of a spider at the far side of the room.
3 Slowly bring the picture closer.
4 Let the patient hold the picture and look at it closely.
5 Put a dead spider at the far side of the room.
6 Slowly bring it closer.
7 Let the patient hold the dead spider.
8 Put a live spider at the far side of the room.
9 Slowly bring the spider closer.
10 Let the patient hold the spider.

Tapescript

Dr John Hart: The other approach, is to slowly slowly introduce the unpleasant object into the, er, patient's environment. First of all so slowly that they hardly notice it, and then gradually gradually bring it more and more to their attention, or perhaps nearer to them physically. So again with the, er, the spider paradigm, if someone is terrified of spiders one could sit them in a vast room, and first of all, er, bring a picture of a spider into the room, which of course is much less innocuous than actually having a live spider present, and first of all . . . that just a picture of a spider at the far side of the room might provoke a lot of anxiety . . . so one would just keep it at the side of the room until that anxiety is allayed. And when the person feels comfortable having the picture of the spider at the far side of the room, one can gradually start to bring it nearer and nearer and nearer, until they can bear to hold it in their hand and look at it very closely. Then, once that, er, unpleasant experience has been weathered, one could then repeat the, erm, process with a dead spider or even with a live spider; again, starting at the far side of the room until the person is fairly comfortable with it in the same room, and then gradually gradually bring it nearer and nearer and nearer. So that with each new step the amount of anxiety actually generated is relatively small.

7b Now tell the learners to work in pairs or small groups and to specify the steps they would take if they were applying the same method of treatment to one of the cases from task 2.

Task 8
Reading

This extract is taken from George Orwell's novel '*Nineteen eighty-four*', which is set in an imaginary future (it was written in 1948), where governments control even people's innermost thoughts. Winston's crime is that he doesn't have thoughts which are loyal to the government. He is to be made to conform by being tortured by what he is most afraid of – rats.

The learners are not given any content questions to answer. Instead, they should be encouraged to read as they would any text in their own language: that is, in order to find out about something that interests them or just for pleasure. If they have problems with vocabulary they should help each other or consult a dictionary.

When the learners have read the text, arrange them into pairs or small groups and tell them to compare how the text made them feel.

Task 9
Reading

Explain to the learners that the cases they heard in task 2 are real ones and that, after the recording was made, Deborah went on a course of treatment to cure her fear of flying. She wrote a letter to the authors to tell them about the treatment. Ask the learners to read this letter in their books.

9a Tell the learners to note down the different stages in Deborah's treatment and how she felt at each stage.

Key

1 Talked about past fears and experiences. (Nice and easy.)
2 Listened to a talk by the psychologist about how aeroplanes stay in the air. (Nice and easy.)
3 Did deep breathing exercises. (Nice and easy.)
4 Sat in a 'flight simulator' and experienced a take-off and landing. (She felt distressed.)
5 Went to the airport to see Concorde and the radar room and control tower. (She found this fascinating and reassuring.)
6 Flew to Paris in a real aeroplane. (She coped.)

9b Now tell the learners to compare this treatment with the one that Dr Hart described in task 7.

Task 10
Learner training

Here learners are asked to think about what it is that causes them difficulty when they are listening to English. The objective of the task is to help them become aware of the aspects of spoken English, or the areas of listening, that cause them difficulties so that they are better able to concentrate on them in the future.

Arrange the learners into pairs or small groups and let them compare and discuss their answers. By talking about this sort of thing together, students are often able to give each other hints and suggestions for getting over their difficulties.

Unit 3 Bumping Into People

This unit is about a road accident. The tasks involve comparing and contrasting how different witnesses reported the accident.

Objectives

1 To develop listening skills of:
- listening for specific information.
- listening for gist.
- listening with anticipation.

2 To develop reading skills of:
- reading for specific information.
- information transfer from text to map.

3 To develop formal letter writing skills.

4 To develop speaking skills through:
- a role play activity.
- a discussion.

5 To focus on the following language points:
- phrasal verbs: *knock down/off, pull out of, turn into.*
- language to make suppositions or to express uncertainty.

The title

The title is a play on the expression 'to bump into someone'. This may be taken literally to mean 'to physically collide with someone', as in the topic of this unit. However, it can also mean 'to meet someone, normally a friend or an acquaintance, by chance'.

Warm up

Ask the learners if they have ever been involved in a road accident or had anything to do with one – for example, as a witness. Let them talk about their experiences, and point out that often a long time goes by before witnesses are called upon to give evidence. The result is that they do not always remember exactly what happened and there are often conflicting reports of the accident.

Ask the learners to read the paragraph in their books describing an accident which took place on 24th August 1986.

Task 1
Reading

Tell the learners that they are going to read part of a statement made to the police by Mr J. McDonald, who was involved in the accident on the 24th August 1986. Mr McDonald was the car driver.

First tell the learners to copy the map in their books. Then tell them to read Mr McDonald's statement and to mark the following points on the map:
- the position of the motorcycle and the direction it was travelling in.
- the position of the car and the direction it was travelling in.
- the position and direction of any other vehicles which were in the road.

Key

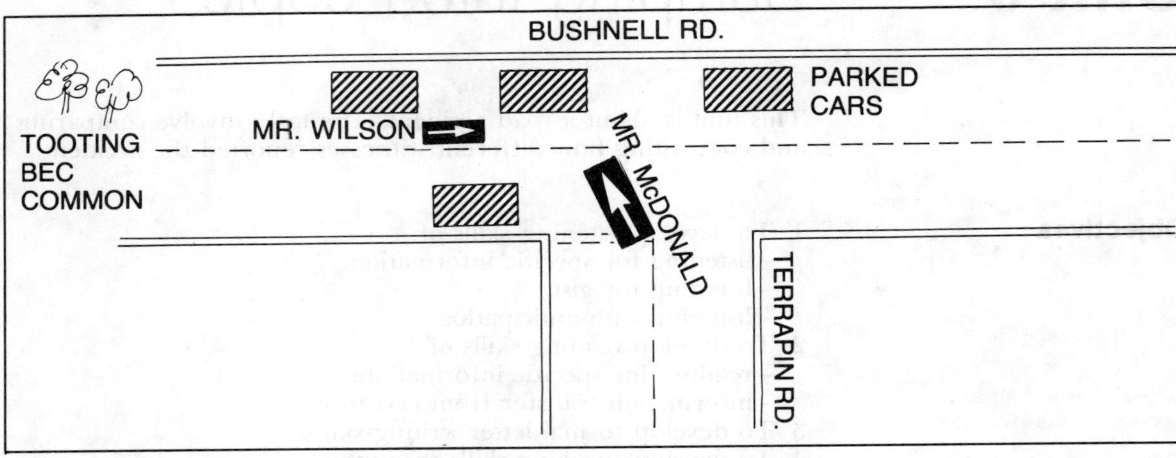

Task 2
Listening

2a Tell the learners that they are going to hear an account of the same accident by the motorcyclist, Mr D. Wilson. Explain that they will have to listen and to make a note of any differences between Mr Wilson's account and Mr McDonald's statement. Play the tape as many times as the learners feel necessary and allow them to discuss their answers after each playing. When they have finished, elicit their answers and check them with the tape.

Key

Mr Wilson, the motorcyclist, claims that:
- he was doing 30 mph (the speed limit).
- he was on the correct side of the road (the left).
- Mr McDonald was to blame because he pulled out on to the wrong side of the road.

Mr McDonald, the driver of the car, claims that:
- Mr Wilson was doing at least 40 mph.
- the parked cars made the road quite narrow (not wide enough for two vehicles).

Tapescript

Mr Wilson: Er . . . I was coming from Tooting Bec Common . . . driving along Bushnell Road . . . er . . . I was on the left-hand side of the road . . . and . . . this car pulled out . . . from . . . a side road . . . Terrapin Road . . . Erm, and it pulled out on to my side of the road . . . and didn't have time to stop . . . because I was already there when he pulled out . . . and I immediately noticed . . . that . . . ah . . . it was . . . ah . . . a left-hand drive car . . . so I thought immediately that he thought he was back in his own country, ha ha . . . and ah . . . so we, we collided.

Policeman: Could you describe the car?

Mr Wilson: Yes, it was a red Citroen.

Policeman: Could you describe the driver?

Mr Wilson: Yes . . . erm . . . medium height with blond hair, moustache . . . ah . . . quite a dark complexion . . . and he was wearing a blue pullover . . . white shirt.

Policeman: Would you recognise him again?

Mr Wilson: Oh yes. Definitely.
Policeman: Erm, what speed were you travelling?
Mr Wilson: Oh, thirty miles an hour.
Policeman: I see . . . Um, were there any other vehicles involved in the accident or in the vicinity at the time?
Mr Wilson: There were no other vehicles involved. There were a number of cars parked, er, at the junction . . . or near the junction.
Policeman: Do you think those cars might have obscured his, his view? Or forced you to the middle of the road, for example?
Mr Wilson: Erm . . . well, first, I wasn't in the middle of the road; I was definitely on my side of the road. As for obscuring his vision, I'm not sure because . . . er, I couldn't see what he could see . . . er . . . I don't think so . . . no. No, I think it was simply a question of him driving out into the wrong side of the road.

2b Tell the learners to read the police report form in their books and to note down what features of the driver the police would like a description of. Then play the tape again and ask them to note down their answers.

Play the tape again as many times as the learners feel necessary and encourage them to discuss and compare their answers after each playing. Finally, elicit their answers and check them with the tape.

Key

He was male. He was medium height, with blond hair and a moustache. He had quite a dark complexion. I would easily recognise him again.

Task 3
Listening and writing

Miss Smith lives in Terrapin Road and was a witness to the accident. Tell the learners to look at the letter she received from Mr Wilson's insurance company. Check comprehension by asking questions:

– Where does Miss Smith live?
– What is the name of the company?
– What do they want from Miss Smith?
– Will she have to buy a stamp for the letter she writes?

Tell the learners that they are going to hear Miss Smith talking to a friend about the accident and that they are to use the information they hear to write her reply to the insurance company.

First tell them to listen and to take notes. Play the tape as many times as the learners feel necessary and allow them to compare their answers after each playing. Then elicit their answers and check with the tape.

Tell the learners to copy the beginning of Miss Smith's letter in their books and to complete it, using their notes. Allow them to work in pairs and encourage them to compare and discuss their work with another pair when they have finished.

Key

The important points are:

– she thinks the driver might have been drunk.
– the car driver should not have pulled out on to Bushnell Road.
– the car driver had very slow reactions.
– he did not look both ways before pulling out into Bushnell Road.
– the motorcyclist was going very fast.
– the car driver was not concentrating.
– the car was foreign (a left-hand drive).

Tapescript

Miss Smith: I think that the driver of the car could well have been drinking, because I don't understand how he pulled out, when the motorcyclist was coming along . . . and he pulled out . . . and he was sort of in slow motion . . . the way it happened . . . the way just the, the the motorbike just kind of turned over in front of him and, really, kept on going . . . Either that or he wasn't thinking at all about what he was doing . . . because his reaction was terribly slow.

Friend: Yes, but he was driving on the wrong side of the road . . . for him . . . so . . . perhaps he forgot and . . .

Miss Smith: He still should have looked, shouldn't he? I mean, he should have looked both ways.

Friend: But do you remember that time when we were going to Leeds, and I was driving, and I pulled out of the top of Terrapin Road on to Bedford Hill and there was that man on a motor scooter . . .

Miss Smith: That was because you were talking to me . . . he didn't have anyone in the car, so he wasn't talking to anyone.

Friend: I nearly knocked him off, didn't I?

Miss Smith: Yeah.

Friend: I just didn't see him, 'cause he was going very fast . . . But I don't think the motorcyclist was going all that fast.

Miss Smith: I thought he was, I thought he was going quite fast indeed. Erm . . .

Friend: Well, he had only just turned in to Terrapin . . . to Bushnell Road, so he couldn't have really got any speed up by then. There were those parked cars, so . . .

Miss Smith: I suppose the motorbike . . . the motorbike, I suppose was making quite a lot of noise. I mean you can hear a motorbike. I mean, the driver of the car just didn't seem to have noticed him at all.

Friend: Perhaps he was tired.

Miss Smith: I think maybe he'd been drinking. But he certainly wasn't concentrating . . .

Task 4
Role play

Divide the class into two groups. One group will be Snatch and Leggit, the insurance company which is representing Mr Wilson. The other group will be McKillet and Skinnet Ins. Co., Mr McDonald's insurance company. Using all the evidence presented in this unit, the groups must decide who is to pay for the damage to the vehicles (the cost is shown on the bills from the two garages).

Stage 1
Give each group a chance to discuss their case together. Tell them to decide who is to pay and to make a list of all the arguments supporting their decision.

Stage 2
This may be approached in one of two ways. Either the two groups exchange letters, or they elect a spokesperson to represent their interests and set up a debate.

Task 5
Language focus

The objective of this task is to focus on the following phrasal verbs:
knock off, *knock down*, *pull out of* and *turn into*.
First check that the learners understand the meaning of the verbs and play the tape again if they are not sure. Then tell them to use the verbs to describe what is happening in the pictures in their books. This may be done with the learners working in pairs or as a whole class activity.

Task 6
Language focus and listening

When they talk about the accident, Miss Smith and her friend often express uncertainty or make suppositions about what happened. The objective of this task is to focus on the language they use to do this.

Tell the learners to listen to the tape again (task 3) and to write down all the expressions they hear that reflect uncertainty or make suppositions. Give an example before they start:

E.g. *Perhaps* you will hear all the expressions.

Play the tape as often as the learners feel necessary and allow them to compare their answers after each playing. Then elicit their answers and check them with the tape.

Key
– 'the driver of the car *could well have been drinking*'.
– '*perhaps* he forgot'.
– 'I *don't think* the motorcyclist was going all that fast.'
– '*he couldn't have really got* any speed up'.
– '*I suppose* the motorbike . . .'
– 'the driver of the car just *didn't seem to have noticed* him . . .'
– '*Perhaps* he was tired.'
– '*I think maybe* he'd been drinking.'

Task 7
Speaking

The purpose of this task is to give the learners a chance to use the language of supposition and uncertainty that they have been looking at in task 6.

Tell the learners to look at the photograph in their books and to talk about what they think has happened. Encourage them to think of as many possibilities as they can and to give reasons for their answers. This may be done with the learners working in small groups or with the whole class group.

Unit 4 Learning How: Learning? How?

In this unit different people talk about their reasons for learning foreign languages and how they go about it. They talk about the sorts of activity they find useful to help them learn and the things that give them problems.

As well as developing learning skills, this unit also contains learner training material: the tasks require the learners to use the information that they hear on the tape and read in the texts to help them analyse and assess their own approaches to learning English.

Objectives

1 To develop listening skills of:
- listening for specific information.
- listening with anticipation.

2 To develop the reading skill of:
- reading for specific information.

3 To develop speaking skills through:
- carrying out a class survey.
- discussion.

4 To develop learning skills through:
- becoming aware of, and analysing reasons for, learning.
- discussing and analysing learning problems.
- discussing and evaluating one's own and other people's learning strategies.

The title

The first part of the title stresses language learning as skill getting (learning how) rather than as information gathering (learning). The second part refers to the learner-training component in the unit and the analysis of how to learn.

Task 1
Reading and warm up

First ask the class if they think it is important to learn a foreign language, and why. This should be a very brief activity – invite a few answers and then move on to the reading activity. Tell the learners to scan the text in their books and to find out why the writer feels that it is important to learn languages.

Key

In order to be able to promote overseas trade.

Task 2
Speaking

The purpose of this activity is to get the learners thinking about the topic of the unit, especially of the first listening task, and tuned in to the kind of language they are going to hear.

If it is possible, encourage the learners to stand up and to circulate round the class to do this activity. It is important that they talk to as many other learners as they can in, say, five or ten minutes so that they can end up with a reasonably long list of reasons for learning English. They will use this list for the following listening task.

Task 3
Listening and reading

This task is closely linked to the previous one as the learners are now going to hear different people on the tape talking about their reasons for learning foreign languages. The task involves listening for two things: the languages the people study and their reasons for studying them.

Before playing the tape, tell the learners to read the short text entitled 'Which Languages?' in their books and to notice which languages people in Britain feel are the most useful for overseas trade. Then explain that, as they listen, they must note down those languages in the article which the speakers mention and the reasons the speakers give for studying them. Point out that if any of the reasons given are on the list they compiled in task 2, they need only check them off rather than writing them down again.

Play the tape as many times as the learners feel necessary and allow them to discuss their answers after each playing. Finally, elicit their answers and check them with the tape.

Key

1 *Donald*: Spanish – for work (his company wanted him to).
2 *Simon*: does not mention which language. For holiday and to meet people (as social entrée).
3 *Brenda*: Greek – to travel in Greece. (Greek is not mentioned in the article.)
4 *Peter*: Russian – because going on a trip there – so as not to get lost.
5 *Richard*: German – to study science.

Tapescript

1

Donald: Well, I was working for a company which wanted to expand its contacts with Central and South America and also with Spain itself, and so they told me to learn Spanish.

2

Simon: Well, I'd, I'd no intention of learning the language; I was only going to the country for a couple of weeks. Er, but I did what I like to do which is learn, um, some relevant and some irrelevant bits of the language, um; and in that it provided on several occasions a sort of social entrée, it was successful and, er, certainly I found it fun.

3

Brenda: I decided to learn Greek because my husband and I were travelling, planning to travel, and end up in Greece.

4

Peter: Well, I'm going to do a trip to the Soviet Union in a few weeks' time, and I want to make sure that I'm not lost and that I know at least where I'm going.

5

Richard: Well, I decided to go eventually to a Polytechnic, to do a degree in biology. And, I suppose by that time, I . . . it occurred to me that, er, many people had studied, erm, other languages and I never had. Erm, and I thought that perhaps German would be relevant to someone doing a science degree, as a lot of papers are written in German, erm, and there was provision for it at the college.

Task 4
Reading

This task is to develop reading skills and to give learners the chance to compare foreign language learning in England with the learning of English in their own country.

Tell the learners to work in pairs or small groups and to discuss their answers together. Then, with the class as a whole, invite the learners to report back. However, this should not be forced. If a discussion does not develop naturally, move on to task 5.

Task 5
Listening

This is a follow-up to the previous reading task: Muriel and David talk about why English people speak foreign languages so badly. Tell the learners to listen and to note down the reasons they give. It should not be necessary to play the tape more than twice.

Key

Because of laziness and because they do not need to speak them well, as many people speak English.

Tapescript

David: Do you think that the English are not keen enough to learn another language?

Muriel: I think, I think, er, it's partly laziness and partly that, er, they don't really need to. Whereas where they travel around the world people do tend to speak, or at least some people, speak English, so that they can get by.

Task 6
Listening and speaking

The objectives of this task are to develop the skill of listening for specific information and to encourage the students to use this information to talk about their own learning problems.

6a Tell the learners that they are going to hear some people talking about what problems they have had learning foreign languages and that they should make a note of the problems mentioned. Pause the tape after each extract and allow the learners to compare and discuss their answers before moving on to the next one. Play the tape as many times as the learners feel necessary. Finally, elicit their answers and check them with the tape.

Key

1 *Muriel*:
- her brain.
- her English grammar is not good enough.

2 *David*:
- people in the shops replied to him in English, not Swedish.

3 *Richard*:
- he was lazy and not motivated.
- the method.
- did not do the homework.
- did not learn the vocabulary each week.
- was working on his own without other students.

4 *Judith*:
- class went too slowly.
- class was boring.

Tapescript

1

David: But what what is, is there a problem with learning a language?

Muriel: Mmm . . . my brain . . . No, I get, um . . . er . . . yeah, no I think what it is actually, is that my English language grammar, er, isn't good enough, and I can cope . . . I can talk in the present tense, in French, but, erm . . . I don't know the, the English tenses well enough to know what it is that I am trying to do.

David: But do mo . . . when you speak English do you think of the grammar?

Muriel: No, because it comes naturally.

David: Mmm, but isn't that the way you should learn French, too?

Muriel: Probably.

2

David: No, it was a sort of challenge to at least grasp the basics and then be able to use the language, but what was annoying was that when you went into shops or post offices, because most Swedes – or young Swedes – are bilingual, they immediately recognised an English speaker, and rep . . . when you s . . . although you spoke in Swedish they would reply in English, which was extremely annoying.

3

Richard: But it wasn't terribly successful.

(*Christopher*:) Oh, why's that?

Richard: I think probably because I was rather lazy and not very well motivated. Um, it may also have been the method that they chose. Um, w,we used language tapes which were taken from BBC broadcasts, and I think it would have been much more successful if I had done the homework and actually learned the vocabulary each week which, er, I failed to do. And also there was little really, um, motivation going from other students because you tended to be working on your own with these language tapes, whereas I think, perhaps, if you've got more contact with other students it tends to be mututally reinforcing, more motivating.

4

Judith: Well, actually, a lot of it wasn't useful, looking back. Erm, 'cos I thought we went too slowly. Because it was such an unfamiliar language, the teacher was very concerned that we should have lots of practice at each stage, and go over and over each item that we'd learned, and sometimes it got a bit boring; because, given that it was only such a short course, I would rather have attempted more, even if I hadn't got it quite right.

6b Now the learners are going to compare their own experiences with those they have heard on the tape. Tell them to work in small groups and to:
– say whether they have experienced any of the same problems.
– talk about any other problems that they have experienced or can think of.
– try to devise ways of overcoming some of these language learning problems.

By talking about their learning problems in this way, learners are less likely to feel isolated or left out, and they can often discover ways of overcoming their difficulties that they would never have thought of on their own.

Task 7
Reading and speaking

The objective of this task is to encourage the learners to think more about how they learn, this time with the focus on how they see the role of the teacher. The learners are not expected to pass judgement on teachers but are expected to discuss the kind of help they would like from them.

Explain that the two texts in their books are extracts from answers that two different trainee teachers wrote in the final examination for their teaching diploma. Arrange the learners into pairs or small groups and tell them to read the texts, to decide which one they agree with more and to discuss their reasons. The texts were deliberately chosen to represent opposite extreme views in order to stimulate ideas and discussion. There is, of course, no right answer.

Task 8
Listening and speaking

In this task the information gathered in the listening activity acts as in-put for the subsequent speaking activity. First explain to the learners that different people learn in different ways and that the students in any one class will probably use a variety of different strategies or techniques for learning different things.

8a Tell the learners that they are going to hear four different people talking about some of the strategies they have used to learn foreign languages, and that they have to listen and to make a note of all the strategies described. Play the tape as many times as the learners feel necessary and allow them to discuss their answers after each playing. Then elicit their answers and check them with the tape.

Key
1 *Roger*: Just read the book.
2 *Simon*: Take a piece of language and learn it by heart in order to focus on the sounds.
3 *Brenda*: After class, do the exercises with a friend. Read the next chapter before the class and prepare the answers.
4 *Ravi*: Read a grammar book – then test yourself by writing down from memory what you have read. Get other Spanish speakers to correct your pronunciation.

Tapescript

1

Roger: So, I read the book, and it was terribly straightforward, and in fact I only read ten pages of it. I mean, it sounds terrible because I was going to learn a language, but I only read the first ten pages. And I remembered what was on the first ten pages, um, to this day. So obviously Spanish is a terribly easy language to learn. Because all you do is read it and you remember it, and the things I remember are 'Como está?', 'Esto es un libro' and 'Esto es un something else, sombrero'. I can't remember. Cinch, it's a cinch.

2

Simon: Among the first things I always do with a, with a new language is simply take any continuous piece of the language and learn it by heart. It doesn't matter at all what it is, um, what the subject is. Er, linguistically I suppose one would say that I'm interested in the phonotactics, the collection of sounds . . . the collection and connections of sounds; which sounds go together. And by simply learning a piece in which you're not the least bit interested in the grammar, vocabulary, er, syntax or anything else, you simply learn some of the sound clusters that happen, and that makes, er, later learning less complicated: it's one, one fewer thing to have to get to grips with when you are trying to learn the grammar and syntax.

3

Brenda: I used to, er . . my girlfriend and I used to get together after work, and we'd try and work out all the exercises together; plus we used to go through the, the next chapter that we were meant to be doing in class, and work out what all the answers were likely to be so that when the teacher asked us during the conversation we'd be able to have the answers all ready.

4

Ravi: Well, I took one of Edward Arnold's book actually, called *A Simple Spanish Grammar*, and read that through and then tested myself by trying to write . . read things and then remembering them and writing them down. And, as it doesn't have a cassette which goes with it, I can't really learn the correct pronunciation. So, what I've tried to do is to teach myself and then say things to people who actually speak Spanish, and get them to correct my pronunciation.

8b This is a transfer activity to allow learners to think about some of the strategies they use in their learning. Explain to the class that they are going to compare and evaluate all the different learning strategies that they can think of. First ask the learners if they have used any of the strategies mentioned on the tape and if they think they are useful or not. Then show them the chart in their books, which will act as a guide to the different areas of language learning that they can think about. Arrange them into small groups and tell them to list all the strategies they can think of and to decide together whether they are useful or not, giving reasons. In this way learners will be learning more about their own and other people's learning approaches. They will almost certainly discover new strategies that they had never thought of before, which will make them more effective learners.

At the end of the activity, encourage the learners to keep the notes they have made during the task and to try out some of the strategies in future classes. You could suggest that they add to the list during the course as and when they discover more strategies that work for them. Encourage them to compare their lists with those of other learners from time to time.

Unit 5 The Cassette Letter

This unit is based on a series of cassettes which John Greenland has sent to his parents in England while he has been living in Malaysia. He sent the cassettes instead of writing letters or using the telephone and on them he talks about his day-to-day life in the village where he lives.

Objectives

1 To develop listening skills of:
- listening for gist.
- listening for specific information.
- interpretation and inference.

2 To develop reading skills of:
- reading for specific information.
- interpretation and inference.

3 To develop speaking skills through:
- discussion.

4 to develop writing skills through:
- writing an informal letter.

5 To develop learning skills through:
- promoting learning outside the classroom.

The title

The title refers to the unusual type of letters that John sent his parents. Instead of writing them he recorded them on to a cassette tape.

Warm up

Ask if anyone in the class has been to Malaysia or if they know exactly where it is – it would be useful to have a map of SE Asia for this. Ask what they know about the country.

Now tell the learners to look at the map in their books. It shows the capital, Kuala Lumpur, and a number of other towns. Tell them that they are going to hear a recording made by John Greenland, an English language teacher who lives near Kuala Terengganu on the east coast of the Malaysian Peninsula. Explain why he sent the recordings, and then ask the learners to read the paragraph about him in their books.

Task 1
Listening

Tell the learners to look at the questions in their books. Explain that they are going to hear a short extract from the first cassette letter that John sent after arriving in his new job. Play the tape and allow the learners to discuss their answers. Then play the tape again as many times as the learners feel necessary, pausing after each playing to allow them to discuss their answers. Finally, elicit their answers and check them with the tape.

Key

a By asking people at the first café they came to.
b Ismail, a teacher at his school.
c He thought it was 'a dump' (a horrible place).

d It's on legs and is surrounded by water.
e One hundred and fifty Malaysian dollars a month.

Tapescript

John: . . . Anyway, I said this to the headmaster – I had nowhere to live – so he very kindly gave me some help. He got another teacher over, who was called Ismail, and said to him, 'Please find, please help to find a place to live for our British colleague', which Ismail did. We went out in his car. He stopped, er, at the first little café we came to, and just leant out of the window and asked if there was a house for rent anywhere. And the locals chatted amongst themselves and pointed in various directions, and, er, then they decided on one particular house. They waved off through the palm trees, and we went and had a look. It was surrounded by water, this, er, wooden house. It's on legs, I suppose two and a half to three feet above the ground, er, and there must have been four or five inches of water all around it, because it's still the monsoon season here, you see. We, er, managed to peep through gaps in the windows, through the cracks, and inside it . . . it looked a bit grubby. It was very dusty. Spiders' webs, um, dust all over the floor, bits of rubbish here and there. My first thought was, 'What a dump!' But, er, looking around the house, it was in a nice setting. The neighbours aren't too . . weren't too close. So I thought 'Well, we'll, er, yes, we'll find out how much it is, per month.' And we found the owner, a lady who lived, er, about a quarter of a mile up the road. A little bit of bargaining over the price of the house, and it was settled . . . for just a hundred and fifty Malaysian dollars a month. That's about forty pounds.

Task 2
Reading

In reply to John's cassette, his parents sent him an airmail letter. Tell the learners to read the questions in their books and then to read the letter. Then, elicit the learners' answers.

Now tell the learners to look at the map of the south-west of England in their books and to locate Taunton and Lynmouth. Ask if anyone has been to Devon or Somerset and, if so, what they thought of it.

Key

a In Taunton.
b In Lynmouth, for a short holiday.
c They are John's brother and sister.

Task 3
Reading and speaking

In the letter in task 2, John's parents comment on things that he mentioned in his cassette letter. The learners have only heard part of the cassette letter (task 1). The objective of this task is to develop inference skills by asking learners to read John's parents' letter again and to guess what other things he must have talked about on the tape.

Arrange the learners into pairs and encourage them to discuss their answers as they read.

Key
– John stopped for a few days in Kuala Lumpur before going to Terengganu.
– He is enjoying the new and exotic food.
– He has bought some 'rattan' chairs.
– He is planning to buy a bicycle and is thinking of getting a car too.
– The weather.
– There has been a power cut.

Task 4
Listening

Tell the learners that they are going to hear extracts from another of John's cassette letters. Here he tries to give his parents an idea of what it is like living in Terengganu.

4a Ask the learners to look at the questions in their books. Then play the first extract and allow the learners to discuss their answers. Play the extract again as many times as the learners feel necessary, stopping after each playing to allow them to discuss their answers. Finally, elicit their answers and check them with the tape.

Key
– He likes the chichak lizards because they chase away some of the insects.
– He doesn't like a kind of black beetle because it smells bad.
– The mosquitoes don't really bother him.

Tapescript

John: I'm alone in this house of course, but I get quite a lot of visitors. Er, in the evening all the insects come out. They haven't been, they're not as bad as I thought they'd be really. In fact, I find the mosquitoes don't bother me too much. But one thing that does come in is a sort of little black beetle. They come through, although I close the windows at night, er, they manage to get in anyway and, er, they swarm around the light and then drop on to the floor and give off a sort . . . a rather bitter, pungent sort of smell. In the morning, I can just sweep them out of the door; they just die on the floor and I just get the broom and sweep them outside. Or I sweep them down the cracks in the floorboards. It's an easy house to keep clean, you see. There are also lots of little house-lizard things called chichaks, that, er, swarm all over the, er, walls and the windows. Fortunately, they chase away some of the insects.

4b Now tell the learners that they are going to hear John describing three night noises and that they must listen and make a note of what they are. Play the tape as many times as the learners feel necessary and pause after each playing to allow them to discuss their answers and check them with the tape.

Key
The night noises are made by:
– cattle sheltering under the house.
– the sea in the distance.
– the bullfrogs.

Tapescript

John: . . . In the afternoons, I often just, er, sit on the veranda, read, er. I might go off for a cycle ride in the early evening, have a bite to eat in a village called Batu Rakit, which is about three miles away, and then come back. Er, the nights can be quite, er, noisy. They're not that quiet. Er, you get, you get the sound of animals moving all around the house. Quite a lot of cattle come to the house for shelter from the rain, if it's raining. And they even go underneath the house sometimes. I've been woken up twice by, erm, a young calf going underneath me and bumping up while I'm asleep. Sometimes, if it's a quiet night, I can hear the sea, which is only about two miles away. Er, I hear the sound of the waves crashing on the beach. That's very pleasant. Another thing is the bullfrogs. If it's rained during the day, er, if it rains during the evening as well, the bullfrogs, er, start making their noises. They go 'warrr, warrr, warrr'. And it can keep me up all night long.

Task 5
Writing

Explain to the learners that when John received a second letter from his parents, he realised that his last cassette had not arrived. He therefore decided to write a letter straight away. Tell the learners to write the letter, using the information that they remember from task 4. Do not play the tape again. Encourage the learners to work together in pairs or small groups. They should first note down all the information they can remember and then write the letter.

Task 6
Speaking

Arrange the learners into small groups. Tell them that they should use all the material in this unit to compare John's home in Malaysia with his parents' house in England which they can see in their books. Encourage them to find as many differences as possible and tell them to try to give explanations for the differences. Remind them of the sources of information:
- the maps.
- the description of John's house in Malaysia (task 1).
- the photo of his parents' house.
- his parents' letter giving details of weather.
- John's tape with information about climate (task 1).
- John's tapes with information about the environment (tasks 1 and 4).

Key

There is no right or wrong answer to this question as learners can include information of their own, but they might mention some of the following points:

The house in Malaysia is made of wood and built on legs. It is detached. The reasons for this are: the climate (hot and humid with a monsoon season); easy availability of wood from forests; floorboards are practical as they are easy to sweep and they allow a cool breeze to blow through.

The house in England is a solid construction of stone and brick, with a sloping roof. It is semi-detached. The reasons for this are: the climate (cold and damp, with lots of rain and snow in winter);

the dense population of England with few remaining forests; and the relatively wealthy economy of the country.

Task 7
Learner training

The purpose of this task is to encourage learners to look for opportunities to learn English outside the classroom, where they will be able to use the language to communicate on subjects that they are really interested in.

Taking advantage of the topic of this unit, suggest to the learners that they too could send cassette letters to English-speaking 'pen pals'. This could be done on an individual basis or the whole class could be involved in preparing the same cassette.

You will need to find the address of an organisation that arranges pen pals – if you do not know of one, the British Council will be able to help. Once you have names and addresses of people to communicate with, let the learners do the rest. They will have to write letters explaining their proposal to send cassette letters. Once the system gets under way, it should be the learners who decide what they want to do with the tapes: keep them private or bring them to class and let everyone hear them (to check their own before they send them and to listen to the replies).

Unit 6 A Fit Of Keeping Fit

This unit deals with the subject of physical exercise. It requires learners to work with the language used to describe sports and forms of exercise.

Objectives

1 To develop listening skills of:
- listening for specific information.
- interpretation.

2 To develop reading skills of:
- reading for specific information.
- reading as in-put to writing.

3 To develop writing skills through:
- writing a publicity leaflet to encourage sport.
- a gap-filling exercise.

4 to develop speaking skills through:
- a brief class survey.
- discussion.

5 To develop learning skills by:
- discussing and analysing factors that influenced choice of words for gap-filling exercise.

The title

The title plays with the words 'fit' (noun), meaning 'a sudden transitory state', and 'fit' (adjective), meaning 'in good athletic condition', and refers to the often temporary bursts of enthusiasm people have for taking up physical exercise.

Task 1
Reading and warm up

Ask the learners to look at the picture and the title of the text in their books, and to guess what they think the text is going to be about. Then tell them to read and find out why the author thinks we should do physical exercise.

Key
The human body is designed to do a lot of exercise and it needs it.

Task 2
Speaking

Ask the learners if they agree with the text in task 1. Then tell them to find out what kinds of exercise the other people in the class take. If it is possible, encourage them to circulate round the class to do this, and give them, say, five minutes to talk to as many people as they can.

Task 3
Listening and reading

First tell the learners to read in their books the list of benefits from doing exercise. Encourage them to help each other with problems of vocabulary.

Then explain that they are going to hear different people talking about the kinds of exercise that they take and why. Tell

the learners to listen and to:
– note down the types of exercise.
– match the reasons they give with those in the text and make a note of any that are not on the list.

Play the tape as many times as the learners feel necessary and allow them to discuss their answers after each playing. Then elicit their answers and check them with the tape.

Key

1 *Alison*: swimming – to get exercise and to get rid of stress.
2 *Susanna*: mixture of aerobics, yoga and stretch exercises – it was fun.
3 *Tim*: weight-training – to lose weight.
4 *Iain*: amateur athletics (track running) – to compensate for sedentary job and to keep fit.
5 *Bridget*: yoga – because she feels well afterwards and does not push the body too far.
6 *Deborah*: walking – to be in the open air, to exercise muscles and lungs.

Of the above reasons, those not in the list in the Student's Book are:
– To compensate for sedentary job.
– To be in the open air.
– To exercise lungs.

Tapescript

1

Alison: I took up swimming not only to get exercise but to rid myself of stresses, and to go swimming at the end of the day when I'd been in the office all day was a very good way of shaking off the office before you go home for the evening or go out with friends.

2

Susanna: That's right, it was a kind of mixture of aerobics, a bit of yoga and what they call stretch exercises, which is kind of . . . erm, well you kind of stretch into a position and hold it, which is supposed to be very good for you. And it was all done to music – it was very jolly, it was a very jolly teacher, who's very careful you didn't do too much and, erm, there were young, mostly young women there, as you'd expect, but there was a big, fat old man called George who also . . . who did quite well, and his girlfriend, Mavis or whatever, and it was quite fun.

3

Tim: Basically, because I'm overweight and I feel I've got this flabby belt around my stomach and, er, the only way of really getting rid of it is through weight-training.

4

(*John*): Er, what kind of exercise do you take?

Iain: Erm, I take part in, erm, amateur athletics, erm, er, three or four times a week. Er, predominantly track running, as opposed to cross country or road racing.

(John): And why do you do that? Is it for pleasure, or to, erm, keep fit, or . . . ?

Iain: It's a combination of those. Erm, I have a fairly sedentary job, therefore I like to have some exercise to compensate that. Erm, but I also believe in keeping reasonably fit, erm, in myself, anyway.

5

Bridget: I prefer yoga.

(Brenda): Ah.

Bridget: Mmm.

(Brenda): Why do you like that . . . like yoga?

Bridget: Um, because I feel that it . . . well, one of the principles is that you don't push the body further than it can go, so that I think the self-punishing aspect isn't there. Erm, and I always feel, erm, very well in myself afterwards; whereas after aerobics I may feel quite, erm, revived, because exercise does generate energy, but I don't . . . I still feel that I'm, I'm driving myself to do something that is, a kind of pushing myself.

6

Deborah: I'm, I'm going to talk about walking which I've got into recently, because I'm now commuting into London each day, and I found that I hated the tube so much that I would . . . I'm go . . . I walk up from Waterloo rail station every day up to work, which is 20 minutes' extremely fast walking. But I like it. It wears down the shoe leather a lot, and I spend a fortune every two weeks on getting my shoes reheeled, but I like it because it's fast, and it's out in the air – which isn't that fresh but at least its better than being in the tube with millions of other people and their polluted air. And, it gets the muscles going. The first week my legs were . . . my legs ached terribly but now I'm used to it. It gets the lungs going. It's meant to be the best form of aerobic exercise, if you do it properly. And I think I probably am, because I've got it down to twenty minutes now, erm, which I think, compared with what other people have told me, is quite speedy.

Task 4
Reading and listening

Tell the learners to read the text in their books and to note how the writer divides forms of exercise into two types. Then arrange them into pairs and tell them to listen to the tape for task 3 again and to classify the forms of exercise taken by the people on the tape according to what the writer says.

Key

1 *Alison*: dynamic.
2 *Susanna*: dynamic.
3 *Tim*: static.
4 *Iain*: dynamic.
5 *Bridget*: static.
6 *Deborah*: dynamic.

Task 5
Writing

Explain to the learners that the text in their books is taken from a publicity leaflet to encourage people to take up some form of sport. Tell them to read the text and to notice the four different sections. The aim is to draw their attention to the structure and coherence of the text, which they will use as a model to write one of their own.

Then tell the learners to choose one of the forms of exercise that the people on the tape talked about and to write a similar text to encourage people to take it up. Stress to the learners that they should use the text in their books as a model and should include the same four sections in their own text. Encourage learners to work in pairs as, in this way, they will be able to help and learn from each other.

When they have finished, the learners could exchange texts with another pair. Alternatively, all the texts could be displayed on the wall or laid out on tables, and the learners could circulate round the class reading the different texts.

Task 6
Gap-filling exercise and learner training

The aim of this task is to activate some of the language used in the unit through a gap-filling exercise and to encourage learners to think about how they process language.

6a Tell the learners to work in pairs and to put one word in each of the blanks in the text in their books, using words from the unit.

Key

(There may be other possibilities.)
1 good 2 fit 3 fun 4 walking, running 5 slowly, leisurely
6 improves, increases 7 keep 8 lungs 9 cycle, work
10 enough 11 unlike 12 weight 13 better, safer, easier

6b The purpose of this activity is to encourage learners to think about their learning and how they process language, and to encourage them to share ideas that will help each other learn.

Arrange the learners into pairs or small groups and ask them to analyse what kind of information they used to help them guess the word for each blank in the previous exercise. There are no right or wrong answers here – different learners may use different kinds of information. However, by telling each other about it they might pass on strategies that other learners have never thought of.

Key

Although there are no right or wrong answers here, the learners may mention some of the following points:
- knowledge of what part of speech is needed e.g. 1 = adjective.
- knowledge of the subject or of the world, e.g. 4 = cycling is faster than walking.
- knowledge of opposites, e.g. 5 = opposite of speedily.
- words from other parts of the text, e.g. 'It is also an excellent way to . . .' will help with 1.
- the structure of previous words in the sentence, e.g. the first word in the text 'cycling' gives a clue to the form of the word for 4 (. . . . . . . .ing).

Unit 7 Building Buildings

The material in this unit is about the Pompidou Centre in Paris and the Lloyd's building in London, both of which were designed by the same English architect, Richard Rogers. The Pompidou Centre is an arts centre in Paris, in a district called the Marais. The Lloyd's building is the centre of insurance companies and syndicates in the financial district of London, called the City. Both buildings are modern and are highly distinctive and controversial.

Objectives

1 To develop listening skills of:
– listening for specific information.
– listening for attitude.
2 To develop the reading skill of:
– reading for specific information.
3 To develop speaking skills through:
– discussion.

The title

The title will, at first, perhaps be confusing to learners, as the noun 'building', is the same as the present participle of the verb 'to build', i.e. 'building'.

Warm up

Ask whether anyone in the class has been to Paris, and, if so, whether they visited the Pompidou Centre in the Marais. Ask what they thought of it. If no one has been there, tell them to look at the photograph in their books, and ask them what they think of the building. Explain that it is an arts centre and was built by an international team led by the English architect Richard Rogers and his Italian partner, Renzo Piano.

Task 1
Listening

Tell the learners that they are going to hear different people talking about their impressions of the Pompidou Centre. Explain that they will have two tasks while they listen:
– to note down the factual information the people give about the building, e.g. size, colours, materials used, functions.
– to make a note of how these people feel about the building – do they like it? Why? If they do not like it, why not?

Play the tape as many times as the learners feel necessary and pause after each playing to allow them to discuss their answers. Depending on the level of the class, you could either pause the tape after each extract and allow the students to discuss their answers, or play it straight through and allow them to talk at the end.

Finally, elicit their answers and check them with the tape.

Key

1 *Elizabeth and Mike*:
There are brightly coloured drains and pipes on the outside of the building, which is a functional construction.
Elizabeth quite liked the bright colours and the novelty of the building but thinks it will eventually go cut of fashion. Mike thinks it was just a clever joke. He would not like to see it become a fashion.

2 *Peter and Deborah*:
It looks like a factory. There is an exterior escalator to the top. It is quite high and there are good views from the top. It is a revolutionary style of architecture and a focal point for creative activities.
Peter thinks it is bold, lively and innovative. Deborah loves it because it is so different, a catalyst for exciting new ideas.

3 *Chuck*:
There is lots of plastic. There is an escalator, a lift and sliding doors.
He hates it because it does not fit in with its surroundings and because it does not do what it is supposed to do.

Tapescript

1

Elizabeth: I quite liked the Pompidou Centre when I saw it. I liked, I liked the idea of all the, er, drains and pipes and things being brightly coloured and put outside so they're . . they really become a feature of it. But I did wonder whether it was just an idea that will, will date. It's not, er, erm, gonna be sort of a lasting attractive idea.

Mike: I think not. I mean, I think it works very well. I wouldn't want to see too many buildings of that kind, otherwise . . .

ELizabeth: No.

Mike: . . . it will become a fad.

Elizabeth: Right.

Mike: And I think the idea will be, you know, very much early . . . er . . . mid 1970s or whenever it was built. I, I think it was a good joke, a one-off joke, and I think . . .

Elizabeth: Yeah.

Mike: . . . it works very well.

Elizabeth: Absolutely.

Mike: I . . .

Elizabeth: Yes.

Mike: . . . wouldn't want to see it become a fashion and it, it done too often, because it will become hackneyed like any other, erm . . .

Elizabeth: Absolutely.

Mike: . . . good idea.

Elizabeth: Yes, it was just of its time.

Mike: Of its time, and, erm . . .

Elizabeth: But, er, not a whole style.

Mike: Brilliantly done. Something entirely original, functional. It works, it . . .

Elizabeth: Mmm.

Mike: It houses what it's meant to house, but would not want to see it become a fashion or a fad.

2

Deborah: The first time I saw it I went right round the back thinking it was the back of a factory, and never realising it was the Pompidou Centre . . . until about twelve months later; and I loved it too because it is so different. And I particularly like the street performers, outside. And one of the best things about it is the outside escalator which lets you get right up to the top and have a good view over Paris, which is actually just as nice as going to the top of the Eiffel Tower and much cheaper and more fun. Anyway, in my opinion . . .

Peter: Yes, I've met people who hate it because it looks to be a bit like a, a factory or a some sort of chemical works. But I think it's . . in my opinion, its bold and lively architecture which stands out and says something new about this century and the buildings that should . . . be there for us this century to live in and to think about in the future. Ah, um, I think art also should have a place that is lively, welcoming, and innovative.

Deborah: Mmm, I think really what I most like about it is the way that it's such a focal point in Paris for young, fun things. And interesting things. Er, people lying on beds of glass; and and it's near the new shopping centre as well, which is just an interesting place to be.

3

Chuck: Well, it's notoriously ugly. (Yeah.) It doesn't fit in with its surroundings. You can see the way they destroyed a large part of the Marais in order to build it. It's a building that has no relation to its environment at all. In fact, it's deliberately defiant. And I think that that's something that a building devoted to the arts should never be. It's supposed to work with the community, not against it. The only reason I . . . well I don't like it at all but the only reason I might find it interesting is as a monument to sort of technology gone awry. The plastic palace of the nineteen-seventies, with escalators that don't work and lifts that break and automatic sliding plastic doors that don't function properly. (Yeah.) So, perhaps it's the perfect specimen of its, of its day.

Task 2
Speaking

Arrange the learners into small groups if possible. Tell them to:
- find out if anyone in their group has been to the Pompidou Centre, and if so, what they thought of it.
- discuss whether they would like a similar building in their town.

Encourage them to give reasons for their opinions. When they have finished, each group could be asked to give a short report of the discussion.

Task 3
Reading

Ask whether anyone in the class has visited the City in London or knows anything about it. Explain that it is the financial centre of London – where there are banks, trading companies, etc. – and that most of the commodities markets, finance houses and insurance markets are situated there. Almost all the insurance markets are housed under the roof of Lloyd's, a huge market floor devoted to the insurance business. Lloyd's is not an insurance company as such, but more a club in which insurance companies and syndicates meet and do business. In 1980 it had outgrown its premises and began work on a new building which was designed by Richard Rogers, the architect who designed the Pompidou Centre.

Ask the learners to work in pairs. Tell them to read the two texts in their books and to discuss why Richard Rogers was chosen for the project.

Key

Richard Rogers was chosen for the project because his design was right for their needs, in that:

– there is one very large room for the 'market', with side rooms and galleries overlooking the central trading area.
– everywhere is accessible.
– the maximum use of space is made inside the building, as all the services are on the outside.
– inside, the walls can be moved to allow for greater flexibility.

Task 4
Listening

Explain to the learners that they are going to hear Philip saying why the Richard Rogers design was chosen for the Pompidou Centre. Tell the learners to listen and to make a note of the features that the Pompidou Centre and the Lloyd's building have in common. This will mean comparing the information they hear with what they have just read in task 3.

Play the tape as many times as the learners feel necessary and allow them to discuss their answers after each playing. Finally, elicit their answers and check them with the tape.

Key

Both buildings:

– are built around a large central room, with walls and divisions that can be moved easily to make more space.
– are quite high.
– have the services on the outside, allowing for greater space inside.

Tapescript

Philip: Well, as I understand it, the Pompidou Centre is . . was designed by Richard Rogers, on the basis that he wanted a flexible arts centre, whereby all the . . . internal walls and internal . . . exhibitions that took place could be fully adaptable; and so the easiest way of doing that is obviously to have a hangar-like building where all the services are put on the outside of the building; and so, if my memory serves me correctly, the Pompidou Centre is very much a hangar-like building with a number of floors inside it, but no permanent walls in that building. And so you have the inside like that, and all the services are on the outside. And, of course, I think what makes the building so distinctive is that all those services – the water, electricity, air-conditioning pipes – are painted very bright colours. And that's obviously what makes the building distinctive, and as a building I think it works. Ah, I think it, it's obviously very different from all the other buildings in the area. Ahm, but I think it makes a, a good contrast. It's not unduly high. Ahm, and it's got a nice, er, square in front of it which is made fully use, full use of. So I think it works.

Task 5
Reading and speaking

The purpose of this task is to take advantage of the topic of the unit to develop reading skills and to encourage the learners to express opinions on what they have read.

Tell the learners to work in small groups. Explain that they will have to read the text in their books and to discuss whether they agree with the opinions expressed. Encourage them to help each other with problems of vocabulary or comprehension.

Unit 8 The Dictaphone

The material in this unit is based on what Molly Keaveney, a business woman, dictated on to her dictaphone for her secretary. The learners will practise their listening skills and use the recorded material to develop their speaking and writing skills.

Objectives

1 To develop listening skills of:
- listening for specific information.
- listening with anticipation.

2 To develop the reading skill of:
- reading for specific information.

3 To develop writing skills through:
- letter writing.
- note taking.
- writing an advertisement.

4 To develop speaking skills through:
- preparing a message to leave on an answering machine.

5 To develop integrated skills work through:
- a communicative dictation.

The title

A dictaphone is a recording machine used by people who wish to dictate work to be typed by their secretary. The machine uses a very small cassette tape. Once the person has finished dictating the work, the secretary puts the tape into a machine beside the typewriter. The machine is controlled by a foot pedal and enables the secretary to type the work while listening to the speaker through headphones.

Warm up

Show the learners a map of NW Europe and ask them to locate the Republic of Ireland and its capital, Dublin. Explain that two languages are spoken in the Republic, Gaelic and English. Gaelic is the older language and is still spoken by many people; it is taught in the schools and is used on all road signs in the country. The Gaelic name for the Republic is Eire. English is spoken in a variety of accents. Explain that the person speaking on the tape for this unit has an Irish accent.

Tell the learners to look at the photograph of Molly in their books. Explain that she is Irish and runs her own nursing agency in Dublin. Most of her business is provided by hospitals and clinics in the oil-rich Middle East. When she cannot be in the office, she leaves instructions for her secretary on her dictaphone.

Task 1
Listening

Tell the learners that they are going to hear what Molly has left on her dictaphone for her secretary, Julie. Explain that they should listen and should make notes on what is on the machine, just as though they were the secretary. Make it clear that they should write only notes.

If you have a language laboratory, the most realistic way to do the task would be to allow each learner to have control of the tape and to stop and start it when they like. This is how the secretary would do it. If you do not have a language laboratory, play the tape to the class and encourage them to tell you when they want you to stop the tape.

Play the tape as many times as the learners feel necessary, pausing to allow them to discuss their answers. When they have finished, elicit their answers and check them with the tape.

Key

1 Letter to J. O'Brien – she gets job in Jeddah.
2 Letter to J. Ryan – failed.
3 Phone *Nursing Weekly*:
(i) mistake Kuwait ad.
(ii) place ad. for Dental Nurse.
4 Jim to fix heater & washbasin.
5 Water the plants!

Tapescript

Molly: Morning Julie. I won't be in today; er . . . hopefully I'll see you in the morning. Would you mind writing to Jennifer O'Brien and tell her she's got the job? 'Dear Miss O'Brien, We are pleased to make you an offer of employment at MEDCO Clinic, Jeddah, stop. A copy of the contract is enclosed, stop. May we have your acceptance in writing as soon as possible? Stop. Paragraph. This offer is subject to a satisfactory medical examination, stop. Would you please telephone our office to arrange an appointment with our medical officer? Stop. You will also need to bring your passport, ten passport-sized photographs, and the originals of your nursing certificates, stop. Paragraph. We look forward to hearing from you, stop. Yours sincerely, Molly Keaveney.' Oh, and we'd better write to Joan Ryan thanking her for attending the interview, but we regret to inform her on, that on this occasion her application has been unsuccessful, blah blah blah. Oh, and phone those twits at the *Nursing Weekly* about the ad. for Kuwait. Er, the telephone number should read four six double six, not four six two six. Tell them to replace the ad. free of charge for one week. And, erm, while you're on the phone, would you mind, er, placing an ad. for Dental Nurse, Riyadh, Saudi Arabia? One year contract, er, salary sixty thousand Saudi Riyals, that's six oh, tax free. Oh, and, er, what else was there? Oh yes, could you give Jim a ring and ask him to fix the washbasin and have a look at the heater? And, erm, we need some more coffee; perhaps you could pop out at lunch time and get some. Er, and remember you get half an hour for lunch, madam. And don't forget and water the plants, please. See you tomorrow. Bye.

Task 2
Listening

Explain to the learners that the first thing that the secretary does is to type out the letter to Jennifer O'Brien telling her that she has got the job. She makes a photocopy for the file but the machine is not working properly and some of the letter is obscured.

Tell the learners to read the letter in their books and explain that you will play the tape again so that they can fill in the missing words. Tell them to work in pairs and encourage them to suggest what is missing before playing the tape – this will help them with prediction skills. When they are ready, play the tape once or twice for them to check their ideas. Then elicit their answers and check them with the tape.

Key

ERIN Recruitment, 43 Fitzroy St.,
Dublin 2 Tel. 334666

14th April 1987

Miss J. O'Brien
Parade Walk
Dublin

Dear Miss O'Brien

We are pleased to make you an offer of employment at MEDCO Clinic, Jeddah. A copy of the contract is enclosed. May we have your acceptance in writing as soon as possible?

This offer is subject to a satisfactory medical examination. Would you please telephone our office to arrange an appointment with our medical officer? You will also need to bring your passport, ten passport-sized photographs and the originals of your nursing certificates.

We look forward to hearing from you.

Yours sincerely

Molly Keaveney

Task 3
Writing

Joan Ryan is the unlucky candidate who did not get the job in Jeddah. The secretary must now write to her telling her that she has not been selected. Tell the learners to write the letter. Encourage them to work in pairs and tell them to look at the letter for task 2 first and to use the layout as a model for their own letter. Draw their attention to the position of addresses, the date, the ending, and the use of capitals and punctuation. You could help them by giving them a few useful phrases. E.g.

'We would like to thank you for your interest . . . '
'Unfortunately, we are unable to make you an offer . . . '

When they have finished, ask them to exchange their letter with another pair and to check what they have written.

Task 4
Reading

Tell the learners to read the advertisement in their books carefully and:
- to decide what is wrong with it (Molly pointed out the mistake to her secretary on the tape). If they do not remember the mistake, play the tape again.
- to ask, first each other, and then you, about any words they do not understand. It is important that they understand everything in the advertisement as they will use it as a model for writing their own advertisement in task 5.

Key
The telephone number should be 334666.

Task 5
Listening and writing

Tell the learners that they are going to write the advertisement for the dental nurse which Molly told her secretary about on the tape. Ask them to work in pairs and to look in the advertisement in task 4 and to make a note of the points of information they think they will need. Then play the tape for task 1 and tell them to take notes. Play the tape as many times as the learners feel necessary, pausing after each playing to allow them to discuss their answers. Finally, check that they have all the necessary information.

Now tell the learners to write the advertisement, using the one in task 4 as a model. When they have finished, allow them to compare their work with that of another pair.

Key
The main information given is:
Job: dental nurse.
Place: Riyadh, Saudi Arabia.
Salary: 60,000 SR (Saudi Riyals) a year, tax free.
Length of contract: 1 year.

Task 6
Speaking and listening

Molly also told her secretary to phone Jim, the plumber: tell the learners to look back at their answers for task 1 to find the reason. Then play the tape and check that they understand that they are listening to a recorded message at the plumber's. Tell them that they will have to prepare the message to leave on his answering machine.

Arrange the learners into pairs or small groups and give them a few minutes to discuss what they are going to say. They should not write down the message as this is an exercise in spontaneous speaking. Then, if possible, record their messages. If this is not possible, ask a spokesperson for each group to say their message to the whole class. The other learners can then assess whether all the necessary information was there.

Key
There is no one correct answer for this, but the following information should be included in the message:
- the name of the caller (the agency's name or Molly's name).
- the reason for calling: the washbasin and water heater need attention.

The message should be friendly, or at least polite.

Tapescript

Hello. Jim Gallagher, twenty-four-hour plumbing service here. I'm sorry there's no one in the office at the moment, but if you'd like to leave your name and telephone number, we'll come back to you as soon as possible. Thank you.

Task 7
Communicative dictation

Arrange the learners into pairs, learner A and learner B. Tell them to look at their own task sheet in their books and not at their partner's. Explain that they each have half of the letter that someone sent to Molly to apply for the job as Charge Nurse in Kuwait and that they have to dictate what they have to each other. But first, explain the procedure outlined in their books.

a First they work individually, dividing the sentences into the phrases they think they can dictate comfortably. E.g.

/Please reply as soon as you can,/confirming your acceptance./

Write the example on the blackboard and make sure the learners understand that they must divide the sentences into phrases that make sense.

b Next they dictate the phrases to their partner by reading each phrase silently, then looking up and saying it. Learner A starts. In this way, they avoid saying things that they do not understand and they avoid saying them in a way that is not comprehensible; it is impossible to dictate like this without being fully aware of the content of the sentences. It is also a good way of ensuring that the learners pay attention to pronunciation and intonation, as the task gives them the responsibility of making their partner understand.

c Finally, they check what they have written by looking at their partner's task sheet.

Unit 9 Character Sketches

This unit is designed to help learners understand and express aspects of personality and character description beyond the simple physical level. Since character description is subjective and therefore open to argument the language of the unit falls into two broad categories:
– the language of description: *dull, broad-minded*, etc.
– the language of argument.

Objectives

1 To develop the listening skill of:
– listening for specific information.
2 To develop the reading skill of:
– reading for specific information.
3 To focus on the following language point:
– adjectives and expressions to describe personality.
4 To develop speaking skills through:
– discussion.
– a communication game.
5 To develop writing skills through:
– writing a character sketch.
6 To develop learning skills through:
– discussion of learning personalities.

The title

A 'sketch' is a brief, general account of something, or a rough drawing. 'Character sketches' are, therefore, brief accounts of people's personalities or personal qualities. The term is often used in literature classes when the students are required to analyse how an author presents different characters in a book.

Warm up

Ask learners to suggest what sorts of thing give clues to a person's personality. Do not go into detail at this stage, as the learners will have a chance to think more about this later on in this unit. Accept as many suggestions as the learners give spontaneously and move on to the next listening activity.

Task 1
Language focus and listening

Tell the learners to look at the multiple choice questions in their books and check that they understand the vocabulary used. This is important as the same words are not used on the tape.

Explain to the learners that they are going to hear Fiona talking about Roger and that they must decide which of the three options in each question in their books is correct. Point out that Roger is a real person living and working in London and that the recordings are taken from interviews with people who have known him for several years. Play the tape as many times as the learners feel necessary, pausing after each playing to allow them to discuss their answers. Then elicit their answers and check them with the tape.

Key

a i ('He's the sort of person who loves making entrances and exits . . . he likes to be noticed.')

b ii ('When he sets himself a goal, he works hard to attain that and to achieve it . . . He knows what he wants and he'll set out to get it.')

c iii (This one is open to discussion.)

d ii ('His mind is whizzing over so fast . . .')

e ii ('He'll come dashing in . . . jumping around . . . He can't sit down . . . he can't relax. He's always jumping up and doing things.')

f ii ('always jumping up and doing things.')

Tapescript

Fiona: . . . He's the sort of chap who loves to make entrances and exits. He'll arrive ten minutes before everybody else and he'll leave ten minutes before everybody else. He'll come dashing in with a bunch of flowers, screaming hellos . . . jumping around. He likes to be noticed. . . . He loves telling jokes. He's a well-informed chap . . . keeps up to date with all the current affairs. He likes to talk and view his ideas on life. . . . He's very successful. . . . When he sets himself . . . a goal, he works hard to attain that and to achieve it. . . . He knows what he wants and he'll set out to get it. As a result, he's successful. When you're talking to Roger, sometimes you're left way, way behind. His mind is whizzing over so fast . . . that you're talking about something, and he's off at a tangent, talking about something completely different. He can't sit down. He's not . . . he can't relax. He's always jumping up and doing things . . . and finds it hard to concentrate at times.

Task 2
Speaking

Tell the learners to look at the photographs in their books. Arrange them into small groups and tell them to decide which one is Roger and to give reasons for their answers. The aim is not to get the right answer but to encourage the learners to discuss the reasons for choosing one photograph or another.

Key

Roger is photograph number 2.

Task 3
Reading and speaking

Handwriting supposedly reveals a great deal about a person's character and graphologists make a living out of interpreting handwriting. Some business corporations even employ graphologists to screen applicants for senior posts.

3a Tell the learners to read the article in their books. Encourage them to work in pairs and tell them to help each other with difficulties. Then tell them to discuss and analyse the three samples of handwriting in their books in the light of what they have read. Explain that one of the samples was written by Roger and that they have to decide which one it is. Again, the point of the task is to provoke discussion and reasoning rather than to find the right answer.

Key
Roger's handwriting is sample number 3.

3b Tell the learners to work in pairs and to give each other a sample of their own handwriting, which they should analyse, using the information they have read in their texts. When they have finished, tell them to discuss their analysis with their partner.

Task 4
Listening and speaking

4a Tell the learners that they are going to hear Dave, a friend of Roger's, describing two sitting rooms. One of them is Roger's and the learners will have to decide which one they think it is, and why.

Play the tape as many times as the learners feel necessary and pause after each playing to allow them to discuss their answers. Encourage them to make notes as they listen.

Finally, elicit their answers and their different reasons for them, and tell them which room is Roger's.

Key
Roger's room is number 1. There are no right or wrong reasons – the learners could justify their choices in many different ways. However, a case can be made *against* the second room because Hi-Tech is dated, grey is an anonymous colour for an extrovert and the room lacks individuality.

Tapescript
A room

Dave: The thing that strikes you the most is, when you walk up the flight of stairs into it you feel that you're in a private house, as opposed to a flat. It's very spacious, very airy. And he's taken, I think, the, the time and the trouble to furnish it to suit the mood of the actual room. The lighting is very much as though you're sitting in a private house. It's very . . . sunny, very spacious, and I believe he's used wicker furniture, which also gives you the feeling that you're sitting either in a conservatory or in, er, let's say the dining room of a private home where you're facing a garden. It's really very attractive. He's used colours like pale green and yellow which also, I think, help this mood along, and it's . . . I, I enjoy very much sitting in it.

Another room

Dave: This room is done in what I suppose would be called seventies Hi-Tech. The carpeting is grey industrial, very close weave, very thin, but comfortable. The furniture is basically square-edged chrome. The colour scheme of the room is also grey. The thing that strikes one, I suppose, when you walk in the room is that everything is perfectly . . . clean, organised. Everything seems to be in exactly the place it was meant to be. Everything is perfectly coordinated: the pictures, the coffee table, the lamps, the carpeting. It all looks absolutely perfect. I suppose the only thing that really is awful is that it all looks like a department store showroom.

4b The learners have now considered different things that express personality: faces, handwriting and rooms. Ask them if they can think of any others, e.g. clothes, cars, choice of reading, taste in music. Tell them to work in pairs or small groups and to make a list, specifying in what way each thing reveals personality traits. When they have finished, ask each group to report back to the class.

Task 5
Writing

Arrange the learners into small groups and, if possible, sit the groups out of earshot of each other. Tell them to choose one person known to the whole class, and to write a character sketch of the person, including tastes and idiosyncracies. Most of the language and vocabulary needed will have already come up in the unit.

When they have finished, you could do one of the following:

- tell each group to read their work to the rest of the class, who will have to try to guess who the person is.
- collect all the descriptions and display them on the wall or on tables and tell all the learners to read them and to guess who is being described in each one.

Task 6
Communication game: speaking

This is an exercise which requires a certain amount of imagination. It is a very subjective task and one that can have surprising results, revealing subconscious connections.

Before starting, give an example to the whole class. Take a well known figure and find out how the learners would see the person if they were:

– a colour.	– something to eat.
– a tree.	– something to drink.
– an animal.	– something to read.
– a vehicle.	– a period of history.

Once they have got the idea, if possible arrange the learners into small groups. Each group must choose someone known to the class and make a list of objects that represent this person. They may use the above categories but should be encouraged to invent their own as well. When they are ready, each group should read out their list, one by one, using the model sentence:

If this person were .... this person would be ....

while the rest of the class try to guess who it is.

Task 7
Learner training

The aim of this activity is to encourage the learners to think about and discuss their own learning personality. It is important to treat everything they say positively – there is no one correct personality and all learners are different. Arrange the learners into small groups and tell them to discuss the questions in their books. Stress that there is no correct answer and explain that the objective of the task is to encourage learners to share approaches and ideas and to let them find out more about learning styles and strategies.

Unit 10 Melody Maker

This unit is based on recordings of amateur musicians talking about the kind of music they like to play and why they like to play it. They have recorded some of their music for the learners to listen to and comment on.

Objectives

1 To develop listening skills of:
  – listening for specific information.
  listening for attitude.
2 To develop the reading skill of:
  – reading for specific information.
3 To develop speaking skills through:
  – a brief class survey.
  – personalisation activities.
4 To develop writing skills through:
  – writing a review of a record.
5 To focus on the following language points:
  – vocabulary associated with music and musical instruments.
  – adjectives to describe music.

The title

The title means literally someone who produces melodies. It is also the name of a well-known British magazine about pop music.

Warm up

Ask the learners if they like music and, if so, what kind they like. Elicit answers from those learners who wish to say something, and then move on to task 1.

Task 1
Language focus

Arrange the learners into pairs and tell them to look at the five lists of words in their books. Explain that they have to do two tasks: decide which one is the 'odd man out' in each list and say what the other three in each list have in common. The second task is particularly useful for developing speaking skills, as it promotes a lot of discussion about the meanings of the words.

When the learners have finished, ask them to report back to the whole class.

Key

1 'Score' is the odd man out.
  The others all refer to features of music that are produced and can be heard. E.g., the musician plays the notes with a particular beat or rhythm.
2 'Song' is the odd man out.
  The others are aspects of a piece of music, while a song is a piece of music.
3 'Duet' is the odd man out.
  The other words refer to a group of musicians while duet refers

to a piece of music (for two musicians).

4 'Voice' is the odd man out.
The other words refer to kinds of instruments, e.g. wind instruments, string instruments.

5 'Practise' is the odd man out.
The other words are verbs that express actual production of music. Practise refers mainly to taking exercise.

Task 2
Listening

Tell the learners that they are going to hear different people talking about why they like producing music and tell them to listen and to note down:

a the instrument each person plays.
b the pleasures they get from music.

Encourage the learners to work in pairs and play the tape as many times as they feel necessary, pausing after each playing to allow them to discuss their answers. Finally, elicit their answers and check them with the tape.

Key

1 *David Poole*: plays the piano.
The pleasures he gets:
– his own pleasure and other people's.
– emotional pleasure and release.
– technical pride.
– the discipline of turning up for lessons and being on show.
– the pleasure of playing with other people.
– worlds opening up that didn't exist before.

2 *Annie*: sings.
She started producing music to drown the sound of her friend's guitar-playing. She does not really get pleasure from it as it is a physical effort.

3 *David Mann*: plays the guitar.
The pleasures he gets:
– at the beginning, showing off.
– exquisite pleasure of producing.
– feeling of satisfaction when plays the right note in the right way.
– feeling of fulfilment when it works.
– playing accompaniments for Annie.

Tapescript

1

David Poole: I would say I, I played every day, er, for my own pleasure; er, I practise and try and improve, I suppose the inference being that's for other people's potential pleasure, er, about two or three times a week. Er, I started having lessons again, er, about four years ago, which I, I don't have enough, but I have them reasonably regularly, about once a month, and that does improve the scope and the range of what I can play: and, apart from the emotional pleasure and release of playing, it actually gives me some technical pride and in what I actually can now play compared with four years ago, which is is a useful exercise. And the actual idea of turning up for lessons, of subjecting yourself to scrutiny, and of practising regularly, is, is a discipline which I actually find quite useful. Erm, so it's been a good thing. And now that I've got a certain standard of proficiency, I can also play with other musicians; and I play with a friend, erm, erm, who also plays the piano so we play duets, and I play with other friends. I've got one friend who plays the clarinet; and another friend who plays the oboe, the viola, the cello; and so I've been able to take part in, in trios, and quartets, and that's, er, not only increased the range of music I play, but actually increased the range of music I'm interested in and the things I listen to, the concerts I go to, the records I buy. Er, and it's opened worlds for me which didn't exist four or five years ago. So that's been a good thing.

2 and 3

Annie: Well for me it's rather difficult to say why I enjoy producing music; perhaps it's easier to say why I started producing music, and that was because, at the time, which was in Brussels, I had a friend who was very fond of playing the guitar and singing but made such a horrible noise that I used to sing and join in in order to drown the sound, and from that start I just continued to sing. And I've been singing for quite a few years now. What about you, David?

David Mann: I think I start, I think I have to confess that I started being interested in producing music purely out of . . through my own ego. Just to, you know, to show off, basically. But I think later I started to discover all sorts of extraordinary delights in the actual experience of producing rather than just listening. I mean I, I absolutely adore listening to some types of music, but the actual making of music – playing it – er, sometimes has brought me, erm, exquisite pleasure at times, quite honestly, er, a feeling of, um . . Sometimes just single notes, just the right note played in the right way brings me a marvellous feeling of satisfaction. Perhaps it's different for an instrumentalist.

Annie: Mmm, I can't say that I ever experience exquisite pleasure from singing as, um, it, it's really too much of an, a physical effort all of the time and it requires concentration all of the time. So it's not really a pleasure.

David Mann: Ah now.

Annie: For me.

David Mann: Yes, I know what you mean about the . . . there aren't . . . I would say probably most of the time the nervous tension involved in producing a little bit of, erm – well, I play the guitar. And it's completely different making the fingers hit the right place at the right time, you know, and the, the problem of, erm, a micro-millimetre out is enough to ruin the note. So more than just an effort, it's actually a sort of constant nervous strain to produce music so, you know, I know what you mean. It's just the extraordinary sort of fulfilment when it does actually work. I suppose what I'm talking about, and this is, this is where the problem of ego comes in, erm: I was so taken by the seriousness and the dignity of so-called classical music, which, er, might be better to be called serious music, shall we say, erm, that, er, I just got hooked really on classical guitar. And now, you know, the sort of, the discomfort involved in getting my fingers round the neck of the guitar into the right position is so much, because I don't have time to practise, that, er, perhaps I actually enjoy playing accompaniments for Annie.

Annie: Um, I suppose I like singing the kind of music that's within my possibilities, which is country music, and, erm, early rock 'n roll music. I would like to be able to sing other kinds of music but it simply isn't within the possibilities of my voice.

Task 3
Speaking

The aim of this task is to get the learners to talk about their own opinions about music. Tell the learners to talk to as many people in the class as they can, in say, ten minutes, and to find out what kind of music people like and why, whether they play an instrument, which one, etc. If possible, learners should be encouraged to stand up and circulate round the classroom to do this.

At the end of the time allowed, ask a few questions about different learners in the class.

Task 4
Listening

Tell the learners that David Poole and David Mann and Annie have recorded some of their music on the tape. However, before listening to it, the learners are going to hear them talking about why they like the pieces they recorded. Tell the learners to listen and to do two things:

a make a note of the reasons the people like the piece of music they chose to play.
b write down all the adjectives they used to describe the piece.

Play the tape as many times as the learners feel necessary, pausing after each playing to allow them to discuss their answers. Finally, elicit their answers and check them with the tape.

Key

David Poole
He likes it because:
– Mendelssohn has always held an interest for him.
– Mendelssohn is romantic.
– he liked him when he was very young and just learning to play the piano.
– he can play it without too much effort.
– it's very beautiful.
– it's a beautiful tune and very peaceful.
– it helps him wind down at the end of the day.

The adjectives:
romantic beautiful lovely simple intricate interesting complicated peaceful

Annie and David Mann
Annie likes it:
– in relation to David.
– because it suits two voices and an acoustic guitar; it is a simple little melody.
– because it suits the way they are singing at the moment.

David likes it:
– because you can play it easily without having to practise a lot.

The adjectives:
simple sweet easy nice effective

Tapescript

David Poole: I think . . . er . . . my, my proficiency . . . er . . . in music really is . . . is, is moderate to slightly good, I suspect. Erm, and Mendelssohn, er, has always held, er, a particular . . . he's, he's, er . . . sort of interest for me. He's very romantic and um he. . . . I've played some of his simpler pieces when I was very little, learning the piano when I was about nine years old, and I liked them then. Er, I've come back to this particular book of music which is called 'Song without Words' because I can play most of them if I put my mind to it. Er, and with not too much effort you get a reasonable standard of performance. They're very, very beautiful and they have lovely, lovely tunes. Er, but they're not too simple that it's boring; er, the piece that I might play if you ask me nicely, er, is, is quite intricate because in the right hand you have a beat of four, er, in the left hand you have triplets, i.e. beats of three, and to get those two against one another is quite interesting. And on good days I can play it, er, and on bad days I can't, so you'll see whether it is a good or bad day when you listen to it. But, although it's quite complicated, it absolutely is is a very beautiful tune and it's very peaceful, er, if it comes off, and sometimes at the end of a busy day and I rush in and before my bath and before my first drink I actually like to play this 'cos it helps me to wind down.

Annie: Erm, I, I don't know if I like the particular song in relation to liking music, but I like it in relation to David and I singing together because it's a very simple little melody and it, um, is very sweet and it suits two voices and an, an acoustic guitar. So I like it because it suits the way we're singing at the moment, rather than as a, a song.

David Mann: Yeah and it sort of mm suits me I suppose in a way because, erm, you can kind of bring it out at the drop of a hat without too much practice. It's the sort of song that's easy enough and sounds nice enough to be sort of effective at a party, you know, but without, without having to spend a lot of time keeping it up, keeping the practice up.

Task 5
Listening and speaking

Now tell the learners that they are going to listen to the music and that they will have to say what they think of it. Arrange them into small groups. First play David Poole's piece and allow them to discuss their opinions. When they have finished, ask each group to report back to the whole class. Then play Annie and David's piece and follow the same procedure as before.

Tapescript

1 David Poole playing the piano.
2 Annie singing and David Mann singing and playing the guitar.

Task 6
Reading

Tell the learners to read the review in their books and to make a note of all the adjectives in it. Tell them to work in pairs, and encourage them to help each other with problems of vocabulary. When they have finished, ask them to check whether any of the adjectives they have found are the same, or mean the same, as the ones they listed for task 4. Ask them to classify them according to whether they are positive or negative.

Task 7
Writing

The objective of this task is to encourage the learners to use the language they have come across in this unit. Tell them to work in pairs and to choose a record that they like. Explain that they have to write a short review of it, using the review in task 6 as a model. When they have finished, ask them to exchange their review with that of another pair and to read and comment on it.

Unit 11 Read All About It

This unit is about the news, and it involves the learners in listening to news reports from the radio and comparing these with the same news items reported in newspapers. The learners will also get practice at understanding and interpreting newspaper and radio headlines. Finally, their attention is drawn to how to get extra listening practice by tuning into BBC English by Radio lessons.

Objectives

1 To develop listening skills of:
- listening for specific information.
- listening for gist.
- interpretation and inference.
- listening with anticipation.
- intensive listening.

2 To develop reading skills of:
- reading for specific information.
- interpretation.

3 To develop speaking skills through:
- discussion and analysis of facts.
- preparation of a radio news programme.

4 To develop writing skills through:
- preparing a script for the radio news.

5 To focus on the language of newspaper headlines.

6 To develop learning skills through:
- finding out how to practise listening skills outside the classroom.

The title

The title is a common phrase which street newspaper-sellers call out along with the most important news headline of the day to attract people to buy a newspaper.

Task 1
Reading and warm up

This task introduces the learners to the topic of the unit and prepares them for the following listening activity. Tell the learners to look at the headlines in their books and to try to guess what the articles might be about. Encourage them to work in pairs and to discuss their answers with their partner. Then, with the whole class, elicit some of their answers. However, do not correct or comment on them as the next task involves checking their guesses with the same news items reported on the radio.

Task 2
Listening

Tell the learners that they are going to hear a news bulletin broadcast on the same day as the newspaper headlines were published. They must listen and:
- decide if the radio reported the same news items as the newspaper.
- match the newspaper headlines with the news items they hear

and check their predictions about the topics. Point out that not all the items in the newspaper may be reported on the radio. Stress that it is not necessary to listen for detail.

Key

Radio news item 1 matches newspaper headline 3
Radio news item 2 matches newspaper headline 5
Radio news item 3 matches newspaper headline 2
Radio news item 4 matches newspaper headline 7
Radio news item 5 matches newspaper headline 4

Tapescript

British Rail Engineering today announced it's to cut 5,900 jobs in a restructuring programme over the next three years. This is in addition to 1,750 job losses which have already been confirmed. Worst hit will be Doncaster, where the current work force of 3,100 will be reduced to 1,690. At Wolverton, in Milton Keynes, the work force there will drop from nearly 2,000 to under 850.

Mrs Thatcher has told MPs that she totally and utterly condemns yesterday's raids by South Africa on targets in Zimbabwe, Botswana and Zambia. She rejected a call from the Labour leader, Neil Kinnock, for economic sanctions against Pretoria. Mrs Thatcher said the Commonwealth Eminent Persons Group, trying to secure lasting peace in South Africa, had discussed the way ahead with South African ministers after the raids. She said it was possible, just possible, that the group may still continue its work.

We've just heard that the Home Secretary, Douglas Hurd, has announced increases in police manpower. It will mean the recruitment of about 3,200 police officers in England and Wales over the next few years. Mr Hurd also said that the Metropolitan Police Force is to be reorganised in such a way that more than 1,000 police officers will be freed for operational duties.

Police in the Irish Republic are investigating a multi-million-pound art theft from the home of the millionaire, Sir Alfred Beit. Seventeen paintings were taken, including works by Goya and Vermeer. This report from Anne Cadwallader:

The thieves broke into the house at two o'clock this morning, setting off an alarm connected to the local police station. The police called to the house to check everything was all right, and spoke to Lieutenant Colonel Michael O'Shea, who's the curator at Russborough House. He said that everything appeared to be normal and the police left, believing it to be a false alarm. But at nine o'clock this morning, Lieutenant Colonel O'Shea called them again to say that seventeen paintings had been stolen, including a Vermeer and a Goya. The police are working on the theory that the thieves triggered the alarm and then lay in wait for the police to leave before beginning to take the paintings away. This is not the first time the collection has been robbed. In 1974 Rose Dugdale stole paintings worth £9m and was sentenced to nine years in prison. The paintings then turned up safely in the boot of a Morris Minor car in County Cork.

The nine-year-old boy who had been trapped in a ventilator shaft at Dover Castle has now been rescued. It's believed he has a broken leg. From Dover, here's John Greenslade:

The boy, nine-year-old Ben Crouch, from St George's Special School at Tunbridge Wells, was finally eased to the surface at twenty to three after three hours in the ventilation shaft. He fell down the narrow entrance – it's only some eighteen inches in diameter – whilst running on the grassy bank above one of the car parks. The shaft is about twenty-five-foot deep and the boy got wedged about fifteen foot down with one leg trapped underneath him. Firemen were first on the scene but then two JCBs had to be called in to dig underneath and work very slowly to release him. He's been taken to hospital, but as he was put in the ambulance was heard to say, 'I'm all right'.

Task 3
Reading

The purpose of this task is to compare headlines from different newspapers. Some of them are from the 'popular' press which is often rather sensationalist, and some are from the 'quality' press.

Encourage the learners to work in pairs or small groups and to discuss their answers together. When they have finished, elicit some of the answers from the different pairs or groups.

Task 4
Reading and listening

This task involves comparing the same news items reported both in the newspaper and on the radio and noticing the differences. It develops skill in reading and listening selectively for specific information. The news items are ones that the learners have already heard on the tape.

First tell the learners to read the two newspaper reports in their books. Explain that they are going to hear part of the radio news again and that they have to discover any differences between the stories as reported in the newspaper and on the radio. Play the last two items from the radio news in task 2 again and give learners time to discuss and compare their answers. Play the tape as many times as the learners feel necessary. Finally, check their answers.

Key

1 Irish Art Raid

The radio:	*The newspaper:*
– it was a multi-million-pound theft.	– the paintings were worth £10m.
– does not say any paintings were found.	– seven paintings were later found.
– Lieutenant Colonel O'Shea.	– Colonel O'Shea.

2 **The Trapped Boy**

The radio:	*The newspaper:*
– he might have a broken leg.	– he has shock and bruising.
– his name is Ben.	– his name is Benjamin.
– the hole is 18 inches in diameter.	– it is 15 inches wide.
– he was 15 feet down.	– he was 14 feet down.
– two JCBs were called in.	– three industrial earthmovers were used.

Tapescript

See last two news items in task 2.

Task 5
Listening and writing

This task is a kind of dictation from the tape. Tell the learners to read the news headlines in their books and explain that they will hear headlines from the radio, reporting the same news items. By reading the headlines first, the learners will find the listening task easier as they will be able to use prediction skills. Play the tape and tell them to listen and write down the exact headlines they hear. Stop the tape after each headline to give the learners time to write their answers, and play it again as many times as the learners feel necessary, allowing them to compare answers after each playing. Finally, elicit their answers and check them with the tape.

Tapescript and key

First the headlines . . .

More job losses have been announced this afternoon. This time, British Rail Engineering say about 5,000 jobs are to go, including nearly 1,000 at Wolverton in Milton Keynes.

The Home Secretary has announced increases in the police. 3,200 new officers are to be recruited.

Mrs Thatcher has called . . . has rejected calls for sanctions to be imposed on South Africa.

Oxfordshire is to get £1½m from the government towards rate relief.

A volunteer youth worker who was caught in possession of heroin has been sentenced at Oxford Crown Court.

And a Cowley man has appeared in court today charged in connection with a stabbing incident.

Task 6
Writing and speaking

This task encourages the learners to use the language they have met in this unit in order to prepare their own script for a radio news broadcast.

Tell the learners to read the news headlines in their books. All of them are related to the news items they have been working with in this unit, so the learners should be reasonably familiar with the topics. However, check comprehension by eliciting information from the class about each headline.

Then tell the learners to work in small groups and to prepare the script for the news headlines that the radio would give about the same items of news. Stress that they should be news headlines similar to the ones they heard in task 5, not full news reports. If it is possible, ask the learners to record their script; otherwise ask them to exchange headlines with those of another group or tell them to practise reading them to the rest of the class.

Alternatively: instead of using the headlines in the book, you could use some from a current newspaper (preferably an English one, but a local newspaper in the learners' own language would also be suitable).

Task 7
Reading and learner training

The aim of this task is to help the learners to discover ways of developing their listening skills on their own, outside the classroom.

Tell the learners to work in pairs or small groups and to read the questions in their books. Then tell them to find the answers in the texts. Encourage them to make a note of their answers and to listen to one of the programmes at home. You could make it a part of the work of the course to listen regularly to the BBC, or you could leave it up to the learners to tune in when they have time.

Unit 12 Kicking The Habit

The topic of this unit was chosen because it is about something that all learners will have experienced directly, either as smokers or as non-smokers. Everyone, therefore, will be able to identify in one way or another with what is said on the tape and will have something to contribute to all the tasks.

Objectives

1 To develop listening skills of:
– listening for specific information.
– listening with anticipation.
– interpretation and inference.
2 To develop reading skills of:
– reading for specific information.
– reading with anticipation.
3 To develop speaking skills through:
– carrying out a class survey.
– discussion.
4 To focus on phrasal verbs.

The title

The title is a slang expression and means 'giving up the habit' (kick (v) = abandon a habit).

Task 1
Warm up and listening

The objective of this first listening task is to introduce the topic of this unit in a humorous, light-hearted way.

Tell the learners that they are going to hear Cecil and Muriel talking about giving up smoking and that they will have to decide whether Cecil smokes. Tell them also that they will have to justify their answers.

Play the tape as many times as the learners feel necessary and allow them to discuss their answers after each playing. Then elicit their answers and check them with the tape.

Key

Yes, Cecil does smoke.
Justification:
– Muriel says: 'How long *did you give up* for then?' Since she used the simple past, he must be smoking again.
– Muriel also says: 'What's the longest you've given up for?'
– Muriel says: 'That's pathetic!'

Tapescript

Muriel: How long did you give up for, then?
Cecil: Well, I . . . I've been giving up for a long time.
Muriel: Well, what's the longest you've given up for?
Cecil: Well, I suppose I gave it up for about two weeks two years ago.
Muriel: Two weeks?

Cecil: Two weeks.
Muriel: That's pathetic.
Cecil: I know.

Task 2
Discussion

Tell the learners that they are going to conduct a brief class survey about smoking. Ask them to look at the three questions in their books and tell them to interview as many people in the class as they can in, say, five minutes. To do this, it will be easier if they can stand up and walk freely around the class. Make sure that they make a note of the name of the person they talk to and a note of their answers.

When they have finished, elicit information by:
– calling out the names of different students and asking the class to give information about their smoking habits, or
– asking what percentage of the class smoke, the average number a day, the brand, etc.

Task 3
Listening

Tell the learners that they are going to hear four different people talking about when and why they started smoking. Ask them to copy the grid in their books, and then play the tape as many times as they feel necessary, allowing them to discuss their answers after each playing.

Key

	When	Why
Steve	About 16.	Family smoked. To be grown up. Friends smoked.
Miriam	18	Socially. Everybody smoked. To be grown up.
Anne	First year at university.	Everybody smoked. Social habit.
John	At school.	Other children gave him cigarettes. It was: – fashionable. – sophisticated. – adult.

Tapescript

(*Miriam*:) Yeah, when, when did you start smoking?
Steve: Well, I started when I was, er, about sixteen, and I really started because I . . well, I think my family smoked and that really made me want to, er, . . . really; somehow it was like growing up.
(*Miriam*:) Yeah.
Steve: And, of course, my friends around me were smoking and when we, when we left school we'd go over the park and have a s. . . , and have a quick cigarette. And, er, I mean, I do remember when I first

started that I didn't really draw cigarettes at all because I didn't really know how to do it and I didn't think it was very pleasant; and it's only as time goes by you get more and more involved in that, erm, in that process until finally you've . . you realise that you, you can't give up. And, in fact, when I first started I used to pretend that I was so hooked that I couldn't give up, because it was like being a child – it was like being a, being a grown-up. You know, grown-ups say they can't give up smoking, they wish they couldn't smoke and I used to pretend to say that. And of course, by the time it really happens it's too late. It doesn't mean the same thing any more. You actually want to give up but you can't.

Miriam: I've smoked since I was eighteen and I started, er . . as you did, sort of . . . sort of socially. And it wasn't a lot of fun to start with.

(*Steve*:) Right.

Miriam: It was quite embarrassing, sometimes, you know. You get smoke in your eyes and your eyes would water and it's a dead give-away that you've only just started.

(*Steve*:) Mmm.

Miriam: Er. And I didn't care for the taste all that much but everybody . . . people smoked . . . I mean I started smoking a long time ago before anything was known about cancer and, er . . . it was just the thing to do. And as, as you said, it was a pa . . . , it was being grown-up. It was drawing that line, you know: I am, now grown up.

Anne: I should think I started at nine . . . I started. No, I really started my first year at university. Everybody else smoked. It was just the thing to do. And now not so many people smoke, it's . . it seems to me that it was an awful waste of time and money. But my father smoked and my mother didn't so it was always a split thing in the house. I don't know, I really . . I think it probably just was a social habit more than anything else.

John: Like most people, I started smoking at school, foolishly. Er, I was offered cigarettes by other, er, children and in those days, I suppose smoking was the equivalent of drug taking today; er, that it was considered, erm, . . . erm . . . fashionable and sophisticated and adult to smoke.

Task 4
Discussion

The objective of this task is to personalise the language that the learners have just been listening to. Tell the learners to find someone in the class who smokes, or arrange them into pairs or small groups so that everyone is with a smoker, and ask them to find out when and why that person started smoking.

Task 5
Listening

The different people on the tape talk about why they gave up, or wanted to give up, smoking. This listening task involves learners checking off the reasons the different people on the tape give for giving up smoking with those reasons given on the Health Education Council leaflet in the student's book. Learners should make a note of any reasons that are not on the leaflet.

First tell the learners to read the leaflet and to take a note of the different reasons given for giving up smoking. Stress that as long as they understand the reasons given, there is no need for them to know the exact meaning of every word in the text. This exercise will help them with strategies of prediction when they are listening to the tape and will make the listening task easier.

Then play the tape. Depending on the level of your class, you could either pause after each speaker and allow the learners to note down and compare their answers, or play it straight through without stopping and tell learners to compare their answers at the end. In either case, play the tape as many times as the learners feel necessary. Then elicit answers from them and check them with the tape.

Key

	Reason given in leaflet	*Reason not in leaflet*
1 *Liz*:	was pregnant.	
2 *Miriam*:	to save money.	
3 *Alison*:		had flu, sore throat or laryngitis.
4 *Anne*:	was pregnant.	
5 *Muriel*:		had nasty taste in mouth.
6 *Cecil*:		painful to do sport.
7 *Miriam*:		in love with a non-smoker.

Tapescript

1

Mike: Have you ever tried?
Liz: Yes I . . . I gave up, er, nearly two years ago now, um.
Mike: Have you found it difficult?
Liz: It wasn't too bad actually. Part of the reason I gave up was because I was pregnant, which is going to be difficult for you.
Mike: Yes, I'm not . . . I'm not pregnant.
Liz: Um . . . I found, er . . . one of the easy things about it was I gave up drinking at the same time so . . . er . . . I always used to have a cigarette with a drink. So . . . er . . . it was, the actual smoking bit was relatively easy to stop.
Mike: I'm not sure I could withdraw both major props of my life at once.
Liz: No. That's . . . that's quite tough.

2

Miriam: I . . . I once thought I wanted to give it up and this was before the cancer thing. Er . . . because . . . er, cigarettes went up from . . . God . . . something like one and nine to two shillings. Er . . . and . . . er . . . so I thought 'Oh this is a stupid waste of money, I'll give up smoking.' And I gave up smoking for, I don't know, some weeks and I took up eating . . . er . . . and I, for some reason I took up eating apples. Apples weren't that cheap. I used to get through a couple of pounds of apples a day, and . . . erm . . . I was spending more on the bloody apples than I was on the smoking, and so I thought 'Blow that!' So I . . . er . . . went back to . . . back to smoking; but that was before the cancer thing.

3

Alison: Well, I always used to try and give up around New Year, because after the sort of Christmas festivities I usually had something like laryngitis or flu or a sore throat and it was a good time to give up 'cos I'd just smoked too much over Christmas. I just decided one New Year: that was it, I wasn't going to smoke any more, and I didn't.

4

Christopher: Why was your third attempt successful, do you think?

Anne: Well, the third attempt was successful because I was pregnant, and so really smoking gave me up rather than me give up smoking. And I had no desire to go back to it once I had a small baby. But the times before it had been very difficult.

5

Muriel: 'Cos that's the thing when I gave up the first time, it was . . . I gave up because I had a really nasty taste in my mouth, and I just completely went off the idea of smoking and so I actually found it quite easy for the first year or so. I just didn't want a cigarette at all.

6

Cecil: I think that the . . . for me . . . erm . . . the, the biggest incentive to try and give up again – as I say I've been trying to give up for twenty years now – is to take up some form of sport where smoking does make it more painful, so if I . . . I notice that when I . . .

Muriel: You've got to do an awful lot of sport, though . . .

Cecil: No . . .

Muriel: To reach the . . .

Cecil: Well . . . I noticed that about three years ago, when I used to play squash a lot, I realised that, you know, that smoking and squash didn't go together, and so then I gave up for some months; and, you know, I think that perhaps rather than try to give something up is take something else on.

7

Miriam: I think perhaps the only thing that could really make me give up smoking would be to be in love with some . . . with a non-smoker. Er . . . who, you know, if it was a case of carrying on smoking and not being kissed, I'm not sure which would win.

Task 6
Language focus and listening

The speakers on the tape all use different phrasal and prepositional verbs: these often cause difficulty for learners of English. The objective of this task is to focus on these verbs by asking the learners to listen again to the tape for task 5 and to write a synonym for each of the verbs listed.

Tell the learners to look at the list of verbs in their books and then play the tape. Either pause after each speaker to allow the learners to discuss their answers and write them down, or ask the learners to tell you to stop the tape every time they hear one of the verbs. Finally, check their answers.

Key

Mike/Liz: gave up = stopped.
Miriam: give up = stop.
went up = rose, increased in price.
took up = started, began.
get through = eat, finish.
went back = returned, reverted.
Alison: give up = stop.
Christopher/Anne: go back = return, revert.
Muriel: gave up = stopped.
went off = began to dislike.
Muriel/Cecil: give up = stop.
take up = start, begin.
take on = start, begin.
Miriam: carrying on = continuing, going on.

Task 7
Reading

The purpose of this task is to focus on reading skills, using texts which develop the topic of the unit.

Arrange the learners into pairs or small groups. Tell them to read in their books the short text which lists different types of stop smoking programmes. Tell them to try to agree on which are the most effective.

Now tell them to read the next text in their books in order to compare what they thought with what the authorities say. This should be quite easy as the previous task will have helped them to develop prediction strategies and will have given them a reason for reading the text.

Unit 13 Getting Your Tongue Round It

In this unit different people talk about what they think of the sound of foreign languages and foreign accents in English. They also discuss the importance of pronunciation in a foreign language and suggest ways of working on it. As well as developing listening skills, this unit also works on learner training as it takes advantage of the topic to encourage learners to think about the pronunciation of English and how they approach it.

Objectives

1 To develop listening skills of:
- listening for specific information.
- interpretation and inference.

2 To develop reading skills of:
- reading for specific information.
- reading with anticipation.

3 To develop speaking skills through:
- discussion.
- 'brainstorming'.

4 To develop learning skills through:
- thinking about the relationship between spelling and pronunciation in English.
- becoming aware of the relative importance of pronunciation for different individuals.
- becoming familiar with different ways of working on pronunciation.

5 To focus on the following language point:
- adjectives to give opinions about the sound of different languages – *noisy, romantic,* etc.

The title

This expression suggests words and sounds which are difficult to pronounce (and which require getting one's tongue in difficult positions to produce the right sounds).

Task 1
Warm up and language focus

Some of the adjectives in the student's book in task 1 are used on the tape to describe how foreign languages and foreign accents sound, and the learners will find all of them useful when doing the tasks in this unit.

Encourage the learners to work in pairs or small groups and allow them to use a dictionary, preferably a monolingual one, if necessary. Tell them to pair up all the adjectives in the box because, unless they do, some of the adjectives in the list could have more than one possible opposite.

Key

loud – soft
harsh – tender
prosaic – romantic
dull – passionate
noisy – quiet

Task 2
Listening and speaking

The purpose of this task is to encourage learners to use the adjectives from task 1. Tell them that they are going to hear four people speaking different languages and that they will have to listen and guess what languages they are. They will also have to discuss whether they like the sound of the different languages. Encourage the learners to work in pairs or small groups and play the tape a few times so that they can listen closely to the sounds and form an opinion about them.

Key

The languages being spoken are:
1 Catalan
2 Swedish
3 Polish
4 Egyptian Arabic

Task 3
Speaking

Tell the learners to work in pairs and to discuss and compare opinions about which languages appeal to them and why. This is an extension of task 2 and will give learners the chance to talk about languages which interest them personally and to use and extend the vocabulary already introduced.

Task 4
Listening

Explain to the learners that they are going to hear six people talking about foreign languages or foreign accents in English. Tell them to listen and to make a note of the languages and accents and what the speakers think about how they sound.

Play the tape as many times as the learners feel necessary and allow them to discuss their answers after each playing. Finally, elicit the answers and check them with the tape.

Key

1 *Iain*: French – melodic, easy on the ear, poetic, there is a rhythm to the language, rounded, no sharp, jagged edges, pleasant.
2 *Chris*: Danish accent – beautiful, low, sensitive quality.
3 *Donald*: French accent – nice pronunciation of 'h' and 'th', very nice, steady rhythm, gentle, lyrical.
4 *Lesley*: Mediterranean accents – give English life, gestures, beautiful mixture of serious Northern European and Southern European.
5 *Ravi*: Swedish accent – makes her smile, sing-song, wants to imitate accent.
6 *Peter*: Danish accent – clear, 's's and 't's are nice and crisp. Greek Cypriot accent – attractive, fascinating.

Tapescript

1

Iain: I think firstly I find the French language, erm, very melodic to listen to. It's very easy on the ear, um, and it almost sounds poetic ev . . no matter what kind of mood the individual is in who's talking, or what they're talking about, there seems to be a rhythm to the language. And it's rounded, there are no sharp, um, jagged edges to the language so it's very pleasing to the ear.

2

Chris: I think the accent I really like is the Danes speaking English. They sound awful when they speak Danish, but when they speak English there's a beautiful, low, sensitive, very soft quality about it.

3

Donald: Erm, I like the way they bring their French pronunciation into English. They can't pronounce 'h's and they can't pronounce 't.h.' properly. And I think that actually sounds very nice. Also I like the rhythm: they bring French rhythm into ac . . . English – nice, steady rhythm, and I like that too. It's just it, it . . . whenever I hear a French person speaking English it sounds more gentle and more lyrical.

4

Lesley: I think the most attractive foreign accents for me are the Mediterranean accents because they, if you like, import their own culture into the English accent and give it a lot of life that sometimes, um, that kind of – the gestures and everything that the English people don't have – so you get a beautiful mixture of the serious Northern European and the Southern European together.

5

Ravi: Um, I like the Swedish accent because it, it makes me smile and the way it's spoken is so sing-songy that you can't help but smile when other people actually speak it. And it always makes you want to try and put the accent on yourself.

6

Peter: I like Danish for instance. I like the Danes speaking English because, er, firstly they always sound so clear: the 's's and the 't's are always so nice and, er, crisp. And, er, I find that the Cypriots speaking English are very attractive. Er, the Cypriot Greek I think is a little bit different from Greek Greek, or at least the accent is, but when they speak English it sounds fascinating to me.

Task 5
Reading

The purpose of this task is to extend the topic of the previous tasks and to develop the skill of reading for specific information. Tell the learners to look at the questions and then to read the text and discuss their answers in pairs or in small groups.

Task 6
Speaking

The purpose of this task is to personalise the language that the learners have been hearing and using in the previous tasks.

Tell the learners to work silently on their own for a couple of minutes thinking of a foreign accent that they like in their own language and noting down reasons why they like it. Then tell them to talk to another learner about what they have noted down.

Task 7
Listening

This listening task moves on to another aspect of the topic of this unit: the importance of pronunciation in language learning. Ask the learners how important they think it is to try to perfect their pronunciation when learning a foreign language. Then tell the learners that they are going to hear Lesley, a language teacher and learner, talking about pronunciation, and ask them to read the questions in their books. Then play the tape as many times as the learners feel necessary, pausing after each playing to allow them to discuss their answers and to read the two texts referring to question **d**. Finally elicit their answers and check them with the tape.

Key

a Yes. Because if a foreign speaker has good pronunciation, people often do not notice grammatical mistakes.
b She is conscious of it but does not know how much time she spends on it.
c The two ways are:
– listening and imitating the sounds you hear.
– studying how to form the sounds – the position of tongue, lips, etc.
d What the second writer, Tench, says is very similar to one of the approaches to pronunciation that Lesley describes – listening and imitation.
What the first writer, Abercrombie, says is similar but not quite the same as what Lesley says. She suggests that it is important to have very good pronunciation, while Abercrombie seems to be saying that it is acceptable but not necessarily *very* good.

Tapescript

Colleague: What do you think . . . yourself as a language user or language learner . . . How important is pronunciation compared to other things like grammar, or accuracy in terms of grammar, pronunciation?

Lesley: I think pronunciation to me is very important because, erm, well . . talking from the other side for a moment as a teacher: if it sounds good you can get away with a lot of things in the grammar; if you sound good, if you sound quite fluent and if your pronunciation is correct, your intonation is correct, then people sometimes overlook little grammatical mistakes because they're so . . they're quite impressed with the way you can handle the language. So as a user it's quite important.

Colleague: Do you yourself, for example, in Spanish – do you spend a lot of effort thinking about or trying to develop good pronunciation?

Lesley: I'm aware of it; I don't know how much time I spend on it but I'm very aware of it, yes.

Colleague: What sort of things do you think you can do in order to improve pronunciation?

Lesley: Ah. Listening.
Colleague: Listening?
Lesley: Yeah.
Colleague: You think listening rather than producing?
Lesley: Oh well, both of course but I think you have to, you have to be able to copy to be able to produce the same sound, and that means, erm, having a very good ear for listening and then trying to reproduce it the same. Because, erm, not in Spanish so much, but in Swedish was that pronunciation was the problem because the grammar was quite simple. But the problem was, there, however much I listened I still couldn't pronounce it properly, so then I have to resort to looking at how you form the actual . . . to what happens to your tongue and your mouth.
Colleague: So do you think explaining the movements of the tongue, the lips, is useful?
Lesley: It was for me there. If . . . because I couldn't do it by just listening. Would it . . . I think if you can do it by just listening it it's better . . . because you're not always going to be able to be in a situation where someone can explain to you how your tongue moves . . . and being a good listener will . . . will help your pronunciation.

Task 8
Speaking

The purpose of this task is to develop speaking skills and to encourage the learners to think about their own and other people's approaches to learning. Tell the learners to work in small groups and, first, to talk about how important they think good pronunciation is. Then tell them to make a list together of all the ways they know of working on pronunciation. Point out that Lesley has given them two already, as this will help them to get started.

By comparing different strategies or ways of approaching learning in this way, learners often find out things that help them make their learning more effective – for example, they may discover a new way of tackling something that has been causing them problems.

Task 9
Pronunciation practice

In this task, learners listen for features of different English sounds and practise saying them in tongue twisters. First ask the learners to try saying the first tongue twister in their books. They could do this in pairs or as a whole class activity. Then play the tape and tell them to listen for the sounds the speaker finds difficult. Encourage the learners to analyse what it is that the speaker is pronouncing wrongly. Finally, ask them to practise saying it themselves and/or work on the second tongue twister.

Tapescript

She sells sea shells on the sea shore.
The sells . . . the shells that she sells are sh . . . sea shells I'm sure.

She sells sea shells on the sea shore.
The shells that she sells are sea shells I'm sure.

Task 10
Reading and pronunciation practice

This task looks at the problem of English spelling and how it relates to pronunciation. The objective is to begin to draw the learners' attention to the fact that, although spelling does not reflect pronunciation, there is some sort of pattern and they can build up a set of expectations about possible ways of pronouncing each letter.

Tell the learners to read the text in their books and allow them to discuss it if they want to, either in pairs or as a whole class group. Then ask them to list all the different ways of pronouncing the letter 'o', with an example word for each. This is best done in pairs or small groups. Finally, elicit and discuss their answers.

Key

Some different pronunciations are:

s*o*me / ʌ /

w*o*men / ɪ /

d*o* /uː/

s*o* /əʊ/

c*ow* /aʊ/

w*o*rd /ɜː/

c*o*nstant / ɒ /

s*o*lution / ə /

g*oo*d / ʊ /

m*o*re /ɔː/

Unit 14 The Answering Machine

The material in this unit is based on some messages that people have left on answering machines. Learners will listen to the different messages and will practise composing messages to leave on someone else's machine.

Objectives

1 To develop listening skills of:
- listening for gist.
- listening for specific information.
- interpretation and inference.

2 To develop the reading skill of:
- reading for specific information.

3 To develop speaking skills through:
- producing spontaneous messages to leave on an answering machine.

4 To focus on the following language point:
- different ways of saying 'to telephone'.

The title

This expression means literally 'a machine for answering', and, in its formation, is similar to other expressions such as 'washing machine' (gerund + noun). Sometimes the expression 'answer machine' (noun + noun) is used, based on the analogy of expressions such as 'coffee machine' (a machine for making coffee).

Warm up

Tell the learners to look at the advertisement for an answering machine in their books and ask if anyone has one or has ever used one. Ask the learners to talk about what they do when they find one – do they leave a message or do they just hang up? Find out if they think answering machines are useful and why they think so – encourage them to think of the situations where they would like to have one.

Task 1
Listening

Tell the learners that they are going to hear four messages that have been left on different answering machines and that they must listen and decide:
- who is being called (they are all businesses).
- why the person telephoned.

Play the tape as many times as the learners feel necessary and allow them to discuss their answers after each playing. Then elicit their answers and check them with the tape.

Key

1 A nursing agency: the caller is replying to an advertisement for a job in Saudi Arabia but would be interested in a job anywhere in the Gulf.

2 An English language college: the caller wants information about part-time afternoon courses.
3 It is a theatre, cinema or concert hall (it is not clear which): the caller wants to book some seats.
4 A Japanese translation agency: the caller needs an interpreter.

Tapescript

1
Hello, I'm phoning about the advert which I've seen in *Nursing Weekly* . . . for an obstetric nurse in Saudi Arabia. I'm interested in this position or anywhere in the Gulf. The name is Jean . . . Anderson . . . and my address is sixteen Elkin Road, that's E.L.K.I.N., Elkin Road, Morecombe, Lancashire. Thanks a lot.

2
Hello. I would like some information on part-time afternoon courses at intermediate and advan . . . advancéd level. I'll be staying in London for the next three month . . . and would like to use the opportunity to improve my English. Could you send a brochure and price list to the following address: Matteo Damiano, twelve Sidney Street, London SW3 . . . Thank you.

3
Hello. I'd like to book two seats for the upper circle for tomorrow's eight o'clock performance. My Barclaycard number is 4929854296124. It expires at the end of 1987 and my name is N.A. Cameron. Thank you.

4
Hello. This is Christopher Caldwell. I'm calling on behalf of IJK International for Stephen Todd. Er, we'll be needing, er, er, a Japanese interpreter, er, some time in the next two or three weeks. I'm in London until the twenty-fourth. If Mr Todd could call me at the Grand Hotel some time between seven and nine, the number is 937-4085. Thank you.

Task 2
Listening

First ask the learners to look at the photograph in their books. Explain that it is a picture of Steve Todd who runs the Japanese translation agency mentioned in the previous listening task. He is a freelance translator and interpreter and works from his home in London. It is a small business and he cannot afford a secretary, so he relies heavily on his answering machine. He only has one phone so his business calls get mixed up with his personal ones.

Tell the learners that they are going to hear seven messages that were left on Steve's machine on the same day. Tell them that they must decide:
– who is calling.
– what they want.

Play the tape straight through and then allow the learners to compare their answers. Play the tape a second time, pausing after each caller to allow the learners to discuss their answers. Repeat this as many times as the learners feel necessary. Then elicit their answers and check them with the tape.

Key

1 A business call from a translation agency offering work.
2 A friend wanting a chat. She invites Steve to dinner.
3 A friend calling from Canada. He is expecting Steve to visit him soon and wants to know the flight details.
4 A Japanese friend calling to say hello.
5 A business call from the police who need a translator.
6 Fiona (a friend of his flat mate, Sarah) who wants Steve to tell Sarah to phone her as soon as possible.
7 The same friend from call 2, phoning again to tell Steve to phone her.

Tapescript

1
Hello, Steve. It's Nicki here from the ITA. I've got five pages of industrial translation for you to do, at the usual rates. Can you call me back as soon as possible? Thanks.

2
Steve, yet again you're not in. Damn you! I was just ringing up for a chat really but since you're so difficult to get hold of, why don't we try and fix something a little more definite? How about coming to dinner? Ahm . . . next Tuesday? Seven thirty? Give me a ring, now, please, as you're listening to this. Hear from you soon. Bye.

3
Oh, hi, Steve. This is Sunil. Haven't heard from you for ages. I've been trying to call you but you're never in. Er, Mum and Dad are fine and my sister's here from London, Ontario, and my brother-in-law's here, and . . but he can't stay for much longer and he was quite hoping to meet you. So do call us and tell us when you're coming and which flight you'll be so we can meet you. Bye.

4
(Japanese friend calling to say she is in London. The message is in Japanese.)

5
Hello, Mr Todd. Detective Inspector Westlake, Vine Street police station. Could you give us a call on 232-1422? We need your translation skills.

6
Hello, Steve. My name's Fiona. You don't know me but I'm trying to get hold of your flat mate, Sarah. It's very important that she gets this message and I was wondering if you could get her to phone me on 354-2851. I really would appreciate . . . if you could get hold of her for me as soon as possible and get her to contact me. Thank you.

7
Steve, I've already left you one message on your answering machine. Please give me a ring. I want you to come to dinner

on Tuesday, seven thirty. Give me a ring now. Look forward to hearing from you. Bye.

Task 3
Speaking and reading

This is a task to develop speaking skills. Tell the learners to look at the three situations in their books, and explain that they will have to prepare the messages to leave for Steve on his answering machine.

It is important that the learners know what they have to do and that they are given a few minutes to think about what they are going to say. However, they should not be allowed to write anything down. The whole point of the exercise is to simulate the situation of telephoning an answering machine when there is very little time to think about or prepare what one is going to say.

If possible, record the learners' messages. A portable cassette recorder and hand-held microphone are ideal for this. It would also be possible to use a language laboratory. The recordings could then be played back to the class for the learners to analyse. However, if neither facility is available, students can work in pairs or small groups and say the messages out loud to each other.

Task 4
Listening and language focus

The purpose of this task is to focus on the different words the speakers on the tape for task 2 use to say 'telephone me'. Play the tape again and tell the learners to note down all the different ways of saying 'telephone me' that they hear. Either play the tape straight through or ask the learners to get you to stop the tape every time they hear an appropriate word.

Key
1 call me back
2 give me a ring
3 call us
5 give us a call
6 phone me
7 give me a ring

Task 5
Speaking

Tell the learners that they will now have to prepare a message to leave on their own answering machine. Elicit the kind of information the message should contain: e.g. name, message to say that they are out, etc. There is no one formula for the kind of message to be left so encourage the learners to prepare the message they would really like to leave. You could play them the recorded message in unit 8, task 6 if they are having problems.

If it is possible, get the learners to record their messages and then play them to the others in the class – they could even record the message at home and bring the tape to class. If this is not possible, tell the learners to work individually to prepare the message; then when they have the message ready, arrange them in pairs and tell them to say their messages to each other as if they were the recording machine.

Extension activity

Arrange the learners into small groups. Explain that each group has to prepare a message to send to another group in the class. Allow the groups, say, ten minutes to decide on their messages. Again, learners should be encouraged to prepare the messages in their heads and not to write them down.

If a portable cassette recorder is available, one group should record their message and send it to the other group, who should listen and note down the main points. Then they should check with the 'caller' that they have understood the message correctly. If a recorder is not available, each group can select a spokesperson to take the message to the other group.

Unit 15 The Selection Board

The material in this unit is based on the recording of a job interview for a position as an English language teacher. The tasks take advantage of the different aspects of the situation. They focus on both linguistic and non-linguistic aspects of communication and on different teaching and learning styles.

Objectives

1 To develop listening skills of:
- listening for gist.
- listening for specific information.
- inference.

2 To develop the reading skill of:
- reading for specific information.

3 To focus on the following language points:
- spelling.
- uses of intonation.

4 To develop learning skills through:
- discussion of the teacher's and the learner's roles in the classroom.

The title

A 'board' is a committee or a body of examiners, councillors, etc. In this case it is a body of interviewers meeting to select a candidate for a job.

Task 1

Reading and warm up

Ask the learners if they have heard of the British Council, and, if there is a British Council office in their town, what sort of things it does, etc.

The British Council is Britain's equivalent to the Alliance Française or the Goethe Institut. It is a large organisation working to promote 'cultural and technical co-operation between Britain and other countries'. Most large cities around the world have a British Council office involved in setting up and promoting arts exhibitions, concerts, education, technical training, exchanges between Britain and other countries, etc. As well as all of these things, the British Council is also involved in English language teaching and provides a useful source of information and study materials. In addition to running classes, it also provides library services, films in English, newspapers and magazines and information on educational trips to Britain.

Because the British Council has its own teaching institutes, it is always recruiting teachers. Some are interviewed and contracted in London, others locally. Ask the learners to look at the two advertisements in their books. They are both British Council advertisements for English language teachers. Tell the learners to read them carefully and elicit the differences between the two types of post offered.

Key

Dubai wants teachers who can teach English at any level but who can also help on teacher-training and syllabus design ('RSA Prep. Cert.' is an examination for teachers). Otherwise the two posts are identical.

Task 2
Listening

Explain to the learners that they are going to hear a short extract from an interview for the above positions. The candidate is Laurie Thomas, an English language teacher working in the Middle East. He is being interviewed by two British Council officers.

First tell the learners to read the questions in their books. Then play the tape and allow them to discuss their answers. Play the tape again as many times as the learners feel necessary, pausing after each playing to allow them to discuss their answers. Finally, elicit their answers and check them with the tape.

Key

a Young military cadets – low level, low ability, low motivation.
b He is tired of the type of students he has been teaching and wants to teach higher ability students as he feels there will be higher professional rewards.
c The general teaching post in Abu Dhabi.

Tapescript

Interviewer 1: Then you moved out to, erm, Riyadh, er, teaching again, um, young military cadets. In fact, most of your teaching experience has been with that level of learner. Erm, in Dubai, you'll be working with a quite different kind of learners. Erm, a lot of them would be academic background and various professional backgrounds. Can you point to anything in your background that, that gives you experience, er, to deal with that kind of teaching situation?

Laurie: No, in fact it's, it's not that way . . . What I've found is that I've really, um, need a change of the type of person I'm teaching. After, after three, er, and perhaps four years now of fairly low level, low ability, low motivation, I feel that I, I now have to look for something that, that, er . . where the returns are a little better. And, er, I'd look forward now and I would apply for jobs where the level of the student was a little higher.

Interviewer 2: I mean, you, you realise the level is going to be up to First Certificate level? I mean, do you know anything about the First Certificate? Have you taught on First Certificate courses?

Laurie: No, I'm afraid I haven't. But once again, er, er, I think that a teacher is a teacher, erm, and if, if I s . . providing I know, I know the students I'm teaching I'm sure I can adapt and, er, and come up to their expectations.

Task 3
Listening

Explain to the learners that they are going to hear an extract from a conversation that Laurie had with Amy, a friend. They are talking about the interview he had with the British Council.

Tell the learners to read the questions in their books carefully and point out that they will have to 'listen between the lines' or infer some of the answers. Then play the tape and allow the learners to discuss their answers. Play the tape again as many times as the learners feel necessary, pausing after each playing to allow them to discuss their answers. Finally, elicit their answers and check them with the tape.

Key

a He does not think he performed very well.
b He does not know exactly.
c This answer is open to argument. On balance, he is probably a little pessimistic. He does not feel he performed very well and is resigned to the fact that there were lots of candidates, some perhaps better qualified than himself. On the other hand, they were sufficiently interested in him to call him to interview.

Tapescript

Laurie: I had the impression they just wanted to find out whether . . . if I got out – if they gave me the job and I got out there – I could, I could handle it. So from the point, it wasn't so much academic as, as, as practical.
Amy: Uh, huh.
Laurie: Would I, would I be able to upgrade my teaching to higher ability students?
Amy: Uh, huh.
Laurie: And, er, unfortunately I didn't come over very well on that because, er, all you can do is say 'Well, yes, I think I can. You know. I'm a trained teacher. Teaching's . . .
Amy: Uh, huh.
Laurie: . . . teaching. And I'm sure I can . . . do the job.' But . . . when you reflect on that, it all sounds a little hollow. (laugh)
Amy: Yes.
Laurie: You're saying 'Trust me. I can do it.'
Amy: Mmm. 'And I'll try.'
Laurie: Yeah, that's right. And, er,
Amy: (inhales)
Laurie: . . . if the next guy says 'I've been doing this for the last year and here's my, er, you know, here's a letter from my past employer saying what a good job I've done', well, he's going to get the job.
Amy: Yeah. What kind of a chance do you stand?
Laurie: Yeah.
Amy: How many other people interviewed for this, do you know?
Laurie: (inhales) No, I don't because, er, there were people went in before me, and people were there after me. So I don't really know . . . the numbers. . . . Erm . . . it's very difficult to say . . . at the moment there's probably a lot of people apply for a job like that. Um, but on the other hand, er, it's good that I got shortlisted, and got the interview.
Amy: Yeah, well, that's the first step. And then, when will they let you know? Soon?
Laurie: Hope so. It's very, very difficult to say. A few weeks.
Amy: That long?
Laurie: Well, they, they don't actually need the people out there till September, so they can presumably afford to take their time.
Amy: Hmmm.

Task 4
Speaking

Tell the learners to look at the four photographs of Laurie in their books. Explain that two were taken during the interview, and that they have to decide which. Arrange the learners into pairs or small groups and encourage them to give reasons for their answers.

When discussing their reasons, the learners should be encouraged to think about body language and gesture as a form of communication. Draw their attention to the uncomfortable feeling we often have when we are being watched – during an interview, when speaking in public, etc. – and ask them to think about the kind of information body language gives. If necessary give some examples: when we are with friends we tend to have a more relaxed posture, take up more space, look them more often straight in the face; if we do not like or do not trust someone, we tend to stand further away, not look at them directly so often, etc. By talking about this, learners are likely to become self-conscious about the way they are sitting in the class. This feeling should be acknowledged and used in the discussion.

Key

Photographs 1 and 4 were taken during the interview.

Task 5
Listening and language focus

In task 4 learners discusssed messages we can send with our bodies. Here they will look at how to use intonation to communicate meaning.

Play the tape for task 3 again and tell the learners to listen to Amy and decide what she means when she says *'Mmmm'* and *'uh, huh'*.

Now tell the learners to think of other ways of saying the same sounds to express different things, e.g. pleasure, suspicion, etc. Tell them to work in pairs or small groups and give them time to prepare some examples. Then ask them to say the sounds to the rest of the class, who have to guess what it is they are trying to express.

Key

Amy is primarily indicating that she understands what Laurie is saying. She is also letting him know that she is listening and that she is interested in what he is saying. The noises would probably be accompanied by nods of the head, smiles and eye contact. They also keep the conversation moving along, for if Amy just sat in silence, Laurie would find it difficult to keep on talking. He would not be sure if Amy were still following what he was saying.

Saying 'mmm' in different ways is a very open task, so it is difficult to predict all the answers the learners will give. However, here are a few possibilities:

mmmmmm	said with a low fall means 'I understand/ message received.'
mmmmm	said with a high fall means 'Oh yes. I see.'

mmmmm — said with a low rise means: 'What do you want?' or 'Yes. I'm listening.'

mmmmm — said with a high rise means 'Are you sure?'

mmmmm — said with a rise-fall indicates pleasure.

Task 6
Speaking

Arrange the learners into pairs or small groups and ask them to think of other ways we can communicate without using words (they have already thought of body language and intonation). When they have finished, ask the pairs or groups to report back to the whole class.

Key

Again, this is a very open task and it is difficult to predict all the answers the learners will give. However, some possibilities are:
- gestures: using hands and/or face.
- status symbols: the kind of car we drive or the clothes we choose to wear.
- whistles, coughs, etc: a cough can mean 'Excuse me', 'Be careful, someone's coming', etc.
- applause.
- finger/foot tapping.
- eye contact.
- clicks and tisks: e.g. the noise we make to express disapproval to a child.
- kisses: we have different kisses, depending on our relationship.

Task 7
Speaking

Arrange the learners into pairs or small groups and allow them five or ten minutes to discuss what each of the gestures in the photographs in their books means for English-speaking people and what they mean in their own culture. Then ask each pair or group to report back to the class.

Task 8
Language focus

The objective of this task is to focus on spelling. Tell the learners to look in their books at the signing chart for deaf and dumb people. Together with other things, such as facial expression, sign language offers a form of communication as versatile and expressive as spoken language. The chart shows the basic two-hand alphabet used by many deaf and dumb people. Tell the learners to study the chart carefully and to prepare messages. Encourage them to work in pairs or small groups to do this and ask them to pay particular attention to spelling.

The exercise could be carried out in the form of a competition. Give each group a different message with a similar number of letters. Each group takes it in turn to communicate its message to the rest of the class, using the signing system. The group which communicates its message in the fastest time is the winner.

Here are examples of messages to use:

'Do you know what time this lesson ends? I've had enough.'
'Would you get two dozen potatoes and a dozen eggs?'
'I think you'd better hurry home. Your house is on fire.'
'Have you seen my pet tarantula? I think I've lost it.'

Task 9
Speaking and learner training

Arrange the learners into small groups and ask them to discuss the role of the teacher in the classroom. Encourage them to discuss such questions as:
– Who should decide what is to be taught?
– Who should decide how a thing is taught?
– Who is responsible for learning?
– Who should be doing most of the talking?
– Where should the teacher stand or sit?

Learners may have many and diverse expectations from the teacher. Some require a very controlled approach from an authoritarian figure and do not feel comfortable making their own decisions. Others respond to a more open, freer approach where decisions are taken by the group and the teacher takes on the role of counsellor. And others fall into the middle, preferring something of the authoritarian approach while at the same time enjoying a freer atmosphere at certain times. Whatever the preference, the learners' opinions must be respected. Use the feedback you get positively and encourage the students to express their opinions and to listen to each other as this will help them develop their own views of learning and teaching.

You could refer the learners to the unit 'Learning How: Learning? How?', particularly to task 7, as it deals with a similar topic.

Task 10
Listening

Tell the learners that they are going to hear another extract from Laurie's interview with the British Council. Explain that the interviewer wants to know what sort of approach Laurie has been taking with his classes and whether he is aware of modern methods of teaching.

Ask the learners to read the questions in their books. Then play the tape and allow them to discuss their answers. Play the tape again as many times as the learners feel necessary, pausing after each playing to allow them to discuss their answers. Finally, elicit their answers and check them with the tape.

Key

a They expect the teacher to be in control at all times, to be the centre of attention, to use question/answer methods, repeat-after-me methods, and to work on grammar a lot.
b 'Modern teaching' breaks the class into smaller groups, making the learners the centre of attention and encouraging them to talk to each other (and not just to the teacher).

Tapescript

Interviewer 1: Have you used, erm, group teaching methods – breaking classes into groups – in TEFL and can you give us an outline of how you felt it useful?

Laurie: Well, group work as such . . . I think . . . whilst the teacher can do his best to make a . . . a lesson interesting and motivate the students . . . but, but, I have found in the past that, unless there is some kind of motivation from the students, something like group work is very difficult to organise. But if . . . if you . . . if you assume that the students are motivated enough to do, to involve themself in group work, why, I think it's very effective.

Interviewer 2: Er . . . what in fact . . . what do you feel about the . . . the modern teaching techniques which are used in Europe? This idea of, er, communicative aspect of language teaching; the learner centred approach. Do you feel that these are appropriate to the Middle East or what's your opinion on this?

Laurie: No, I've . . . I've not found that. I've found that a . . . a slightly more teacher centred, structural approach works better. From the students that I've had in the past.

Interviewer 2: Have you any idea why this might be so?

Laurie: Possibly it's to do with their own background. I . . . I think that their educational background is teacher centred, rote learning, and that's what they're used to. They're . . . they're unfamiliar with being left to their own devices in a . . . in a sense.

Extension activity

This activity depends on the goodwill of both learners and other teachers in your school, as learners are asked to question teachers about their teaching methods. Before deciding to do the task, check with your colleagues that they do not mind being questioned about their attitudes to teaching.

Arrange the learners into small groups and explain that they are now going to talk to the teachers and learners in the school to find out what sort of approach to learning they favour, how they see their role in the classroom, and why. To avoid imposing too much on your colleagues, it might be a good idea if each group adopted a different teacher. Give the learners time to prepare and discuss the interview. When the interviews are over, reorganise the groups so that there is one member of each of the original groups together in a new group and tell them to report back on the interviews.

Unit 16 A Diplomatic Frieze

This unit is based on an extract from an official taped guide to the British Museum. It deals with the language used to describe works of art, and extends the topic to include discussion of whether great works of art of the past should be returned to their countries of origin.

Objectives

1 To develop listening skills of:
- listening for specific information.
- intensive listening.

2 To develop the reading skill of:
- reading for specific information.

3 To develop speaking skills through:
- debate.
- discussion.

4 To develop integrated skills through:
- project work.

The title

The title is a play on the words 'frieze' ('an ornamental band, just below the ceiling or cornice') and 'freeze' ('a period of frost'), both of which have the same pronunciation. A 'diplomatic freeze' suggests that there has been a cooling of international relations between two countries.

Warm up

Ask if anyone has ever visited the British Museum and, if so, what they thought of it. If none of the learners have visited the museum, find out what they know about it.

The British Museum is one of the world's major museums of archaeology and occupies a large 19th century building in the centre of London. The museum groups its main collections into galleries and the tape for this unit is taken from the portable guide for the Duveen Gallery, which houses the most famous of the museum's classical Greek collections.

Task 1
Listening

Tell the learners to make a quick copy of the ground plan of the Duveen Gallery in their books. Point out that the plan is part annotated. Ask them to imagine that they have just walked into the gallery and are standing facing the desk in the smaller room to the right. Explain that they are going to hear the beginning of the gallery guide and that they must listen and complete the annotation of the plan.

Play the tape as many times as the learners feel necessary, pausing after each playing to allow them to discuss their answers. Finally, elicit their answers and check them with the tape.

Key

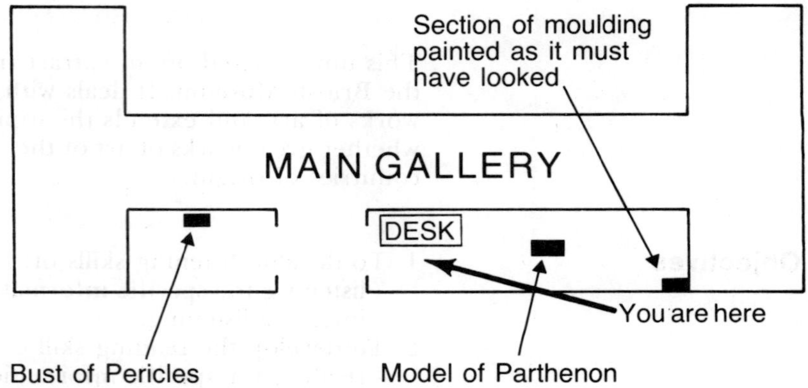

Tapescript

Museum guide: The room in which we are now standing, and the smaller one opposite, contain a variety of information telling you about the Parthenon. Make your way to the centre of this room, where you'll find a model of the outcrop of rock at Athens known as the Acropolis. Here the Parthenon was built between the years 447 and 432 BC. The model shows the Parthenon in ruins as it looked at the beginning of the nineteenth century. It was then that Lord Elgin, British ambassador at Constantinople, arranged for much of the sculpture to be taken down from the building. The Elgin Marbles, as they became known, were eventually transported to England and bought for the British Museum. In the far right-hand corner of the room is a reconstruction of a section of moulding from the Parthenon which will help you to see how the building must have looked newly painted in bright contrasting colours. I shall pause for you to look at it . . . If now you retrace your steps past the desk and go across to the smaller room facing the entrance to this one, you'll find a bust of the Athenian statesman, Pericles. The Parthenon was part of a vast building programme which Pericles' administration carried out to adorn Athens at the height of her prosperity. The temple itself was built to house a magnificent new statue of the goddess Athena, designed by the sculptor Pheidias. If you would like to learn more of the history of the Elgin Marbles, or how they fit into the architecture of the Parthenon, you should now turn off the tape and remain for a few minutes looking at the information in these two rooms.

Task 2
Listening

Now tell the learners to look at the questions in their books, which refer to the same extract from the tape that they have just listened to. Tell them to work in pairs and to try to answer the questions from memory, without hearing the tape again. Then play the tape a second time, if the learners ask you to do so. Finally, elicit their answers and check them with the tape.

Key

a He was a British ambassador to Constantinople at the beginning of the 19th century.

b They are sections from the marble sculpture taken from the Parthenon by Lord Elgin.

c Pericles was responsible for building it. It was built between 447 and 432 BC.

d Pheidias, the sculptor.

Task 3
Listening

Tell the learners to look at the photographs in their books, and explain that they will hear a short description of one of the photographs and will have to decide which one it is. Explain the a centaur is half-man, half-horse, and that a Lapith is a hillsman. Play the tape as many times as the learners feel necessary, pausing after each playing to allow them to discuss their answers. Then elicit their answers and check them with the tape.

Key

Photograph number 2.

Tapescript

Museum guide: . . . Here, a centaur, clutching at a wound in his back, tries to get away, while a Lapith grabs him by the throat, drawing himself up to strike a fatal blow. As he does so, his cloak forms an elaborate backdrop to the struggle.

Task 4
Listening

The tape for task 4 contains the names of different Greek gods and goddesses. To help the learners, write up on the blackboard in random order the names of all the gods and figures that are mentioned on the tape. You will find these in the tapescript. Ask the learners if they know who the gods are, e.g. Zeus is father of the gods etc.

Tell the learners to look at the photograph in their books. There are fourteen figures in it. Some figures have been annotated and the learners will have to listen and complete the annotation. Play the tape as many times as the learners feel necessary and pause after each playing to allow them to discuss their answers. Finally, elicit their answers and check them with the tape.

Key

The order from right to left is as follows:
Hephaistos; Athena; a child; an old man (the Archon Basileus); the Priestess of Athena; two girls carrying stools on their heads; Zeus; Hera; Iris; Aries; Demeter; Dionysos; Hermes.

Tapescript

Museum guide: You're now looking at the scene which occupied the central position on the frieze over the porch at the east end of the building. On the far right are two seated gods, Athena herself and Hephaistos, the lame smith-god, turning towards her. Hephaistos is identified by the crutch under his right arm. They sit with their backs to the two smaller figures holding the Peplos. The child is probably one of the girls between the ages of seven and eleven who were chosen to look after the cult of Athena. The man may be identified as a high official of Athens, the Archon Basileus. On the left again of these two, is a woman who must be the priestess of Athena. She's approached by two girls carrying stools on their heads which are probably for the Archon Basileus and the priestess. The legs of the stools are now missing. Further along is Zeus, a bearded figure, who sits facing the procession which advances along the other side of the Parthenon. As father of the gods he sits on a throne instead of on a stool. Next to him his wife, Hera, is adjusting her veil. By her stands Iris, female messenger of the gods. Then comes the muscular figure of Aries, god of war. Next, Demeter the goddess of grain. And finally, Dionysos, god of wine, leaning on the shoulder of Hermes, the other messenger god. He sits with his flat sun-hat resting on his knee.

Task 5
Reading

The purpose of this activity is to take advantage of the topic of the first listening task to develop reading skills. It is also an introduction to the next listening task.

Tell the learners to read the newspaper article in their books and to make a note of the arguments for and against returning the Elgin Marbles to Greece. Encourage them to work in pairs and to discuss their answers.

Key

Arguments for:
- they are an integral part of a structure that was mutilated and they must be returned.
- they are unique to Greece and specific to the country's identity.
- the gesture from Britain would honour Britain's name.
- England and Greece are friends – in the spirit of the friendship, the injustice can be corrected.
- they are the 'Parthenon' Marbles and their removal involved wanton destruction.

Arguments against:
- returning them could set a precedent leading to the emptying of museums all over the world.
- museums are vital assets and must be protected.

Task 6
Listening

The learners will now hear the British Museum's official response from Miss Rankine, the deputy director of the museum. Tell the learners to listen and to make notes on what she thinks of the Greek claim. Play the tape as many times as the learners feel necessary, pausing after each playing to allow them to discuss their answers. Finally, elicit their answers and check them with the tape.

Key

The central points to Miss Rankine's arguments are:
- in the British Museum they are available for everyone to see.

– they form a core of scholarly research.
– they are not actually owned by anyone. They are entrusted to the trustees and housed in the British Museum.
– they act as extraordinary ambassadors for Greece.

Tapescript

Miss Jean Rankine: Well, there's been an enormous amount in the press in the last few years about the Greek claim that the Parthenon sculptures, which are housed in this museum, should be returned to Greece. Erm, there are lots of emotive headlines saying the sculptures should be, erm, mounted on the monument for which they were built . . . and, er, should appear in their natural home under the blue skies of Athens. The, um . . this museum's position is that, er, the collections of this museum are vested in the trustees, they are entrusted to the trustees . . . and are held in trust not just for this nation but for the whole of mankind, and that to dismember those collections would do a great disservice . . . to scholarship and to public interest. It is also the case that a former Greek ambassador said that the Parthenon sculptures in the British Museum were the best ambassadors for Greece that he could possibly imagine.

Task 7
Speaking

In this activity the learners are asked to express their views on what should be done with the Elgin Marbles. There are several ways in which the task may be approached:
– The learners could simply be given a few minutes to form an opinion and then be asked to express their views informally as a whole class activity.
– The learners could be arranged into small groups to discuss the question. Then each group could choose a spokesperson to present the points raised and a full class discussion could take place.
– The learners could be arranged into small groups and given time, say a week, to prepare a study of the problem based on materials they have collected (newspaper articles, articles from books, etc.). Each group could present the results of their study to the whole class and they could discuss the points that are raised.
– A formal debate could be set up. This would require 'a motion': for example, 'The Elgin Marbles must be returned to Greece'. A chairperson would have to be appointed, and two teams organised: one to argue for the motion and another to argue against it. The two teams should be given enough time to prepare their arguments (say, a couple of days). During the debate, the teams would present their arguments, then questions would be asked or points made from 'the floor' (the rest of the class) while the chairperson would keep order. At the end of the allotted time for the debate, the chairperson should take a vote from the floor to decide which team had presented the strongest arguments.

Task 8
Integrated skills (project work)

This task is linked to the previous one and requires learners to visit a local museum to find out where its exhibits come from. Arrange the learners into groups and give them, say, a week to investigate the origin of the exhibits in a local museum and to present a case for or against returning them to where they originally came from. Each group must then present their case to the rest of the class, who ask questions or give their point of view.

Task 9
Speaking and listening

The objective of this task is to take advantage of the topic of the unit to develop speaking skills. Tell the learners to look at the photograph of the Uccello painting in their books and to imagine that they are responsible for producing the recorded guide for this exhibit. Arrange them into small groups and tell them to prepare the script for the guide. If it is possible, get them to record the script. Then tell them to listen to their own recording or one from another group and to think about the points listed in their books.

If it is not possible to record the scripts, tell each group to appoint a spokesperson who will read the script either to the class as a whole or to another group, who will listen out for the points listed in their books.

Unit 17 Dial A Line

The material in this unit is based on the recorded information that British Telecom, the British telephone company, offers to its subscribers. Learners will practise listening to and processing telephone messages dealing with a variety of topics.

Objectives

1 To develop listening skills of:
  – listening for gist.
  – listening for specific information.
2 To develop reading skills of:
  – reading for specific information.
  – reading road maps.
3 To develop speaking skills through:
  – preparation of a recorded message.
  – discussion.
4 To develop learning skills through:
  – encouraging the learners to look for opportunities to learn outside the classroom.

The title

The names of most of the British Telecom information services contain the word 'line' – recipeline, cricketline, spaceline, etc. The title refers to the act of dialling the number for any of these lines.

Task 1
Warm up

Ask the learners which they prefer, telephoning or writing letters. Ask them to think about the advantages and disadvantages of each.

Then ask them to think of all the different services which their local telephone company offers, e.g. weather forecast, the time, etc. and whether they know of any others offered in other countries.

Task 2
Reading and listening

Tell the learners to look in their books at the list of some of the services offered by British Telecom in London. Ask them to read it carefully and to discuss in pairs or small groups what they think the services are:

Here are explanations of some of the more unusual services and unusual vocabulary used in the list:

Capital Radio: an independent radio station for young people in the London area.
Brain-teaser: a difficult question or puzzle to entertain adults and older children.
Test match: an international cricket competition.
Hits: pop songs that reach the number 1 position in the charts.
Bulletin: short news report.
Leisureline: public entertainment, e.g. plays, shows, concerts, etc.

Storyline: bedtime stories for children.
Round-up: sports results, scores.
Traveline: detailed regional road reports.

Now explain to the learners that they are going to hear extracts from six of the services on the list. Tell them to listen and to identify each service. Depending on the level of your class, either play the tape straight through and allow the learners to discuss their answers at the end, or stop the tape after each extract and allow them to discuss their answers before moving on to the next one. In either case, play the tape as many times as the learners feel necessary, pausing after each playing to allow them to discuss their answers. Elicit their answers and check them with the tape.

Key

1 I.R.N. Newsline.
2 Leisureline.
3 Timeline.
4 Starline.
5 F.T. Cityline.
6 Traveline.

Tapescript

1
Seven of the paintings stolen by art robbers from an Irish mansion have been found nearby, in an abandoned van. At least ten million pounds' worth of paintings were taken from the collection of diamond magnate, Sir Alfred Beit, among them works by such masters as Vermeer and Goya. An alarm did go off in the early hours and was attended by the police, but there's been no explanation of how the robbery wasn't discovered then or whether the raiders struck later.

2
Shaftesbury Avenue, home of some of London's many theatres, is one hundred years old this year. To celebrate this event, the Avenue is to be closed to all traffic today. And from twelve o'clock midday there'll be lots of street entertainment, including a fireman's bicycle race and the chance to view Soho fire station. At three o'clock in the afternoon, the Shaftesbury Avenue grand parade of floats leaves Bedford Square to make its way along Shaftesbury Avenue to Piccadilly Circus. Among those taking part you can expect to see bands and clowns, Pearly Kings and Queens, as well as representatives of all the people who live in Soho, including nearby Chinatown. After a church service at St Anne's in Dean Street, there'll be a spectacular firework display. So, go along to Shaftesbury Avenue and help celebrate this special centenary.

3
At the third stroke the time from Accurist will be four thirty-eight and forty seconds . . . beep beep beep . . . At the third stroke the time from Accurist will be four thirty-eight and fifty seconds . . . beep beep beep . . . At the third stroke the time from Accurist will be four thirty-nine precisely . . . beep beep beep.

4

Ensure the week gets off to a flying start by putting all your energies into your work. Once you get moving in that area, you'll be surprised how everything else takes off too. Ignore any rumours that seem to impinge on your romantic life . . . Pisces . . . you may feel a chum has double-crossed you in some way. If that's the case, let them know how you feel. It's not a good idea, either, to take romantic risks of any kind. They'll only backfire on you and leave you worse off than you were to start with.

5

FT index at three o'clock up seven point seven at thirteen twelve point seven. FTSE up seven point three at fifteen ninety-three point one. Pound/dollar rate, one point five one six one: down forty-four points. Canadian dollar, two point zero seven four four. Deutsche Mark at three point four zero seven four. Dutch guilder, three point eight three nine four. Belgian franc, sixty-nine point five two. Danish krona, twelve point six two five nine. French franc, ten point eight five five one. Lira, two three three six point seven. Peseta, two one six point three one. Swiss franc, two point eight four zero five. Swedish krona, ten point eight five five one. Japanese yen, two fifty-five point nine three. Irish punt, one point one one nine six. Australian dollar, two point one zero five six. Hong Kong dollar, eleven point eight four six six. Saudi riyal, five point five at three five five . . . Sterling index at three o'clock at seventy-six point five.

6

There's a contraflow on the M4 near Maidenhead in Berkshire between junctions 9 and 10, where peak hour delays should be expected. An air pageant is being held at Southend-on-Sea today, which will make the area very congested for traffic. Drivers should consider leaving their cars outside and completing their journeys by public transport.

In London, weekend work has closed the southbound section of the Kingsway until five o'clock tomorrow morning and traffic is being diverted at Great Queen Street to Aldwych. There are still restrictions in Piccadilly Circus, affecting all adjoining streets.

The A12 is affected on the M11 intersection at Redbridge. Peak-hour traffic is subject to d'delay at the flyover. There are also restrictions on the A13 near Plaistow and East Ham areas. In Cambridgeshire, construction work is in progress on the A1 north of Huntingdon.

Task 3
Listening

Tell the learners to copy the chart in their books. While they are doing this, rewind the tape to extract 5. Check that the learners are familiar with the foreign currencies on the chart:

US $ = US dollar.
D.Mark = Deutsche Mark (West Germany)
S.Franc = Swiss franc.
Yen = Japanese currency.

Tell the learners to listen to the tape and to fill in the chart with the exchange rates for the currencies listed. The tape is quite fast, so play it as many times as the learners feel necessary, pausing after each playing to allow them to discuss their answers. Finally, elicit their answers and check them with the tape.

Key

US $: 1.5161
D.Mark: 3.4074
S.Franc: 2.8405
Yen: 255.93

Task 4
Language focus

This task will help the learners with the vocabulary in the next listening task. Tell the learners to look at the sketch map in their books and to match the five words above it with the numbers on the map. Encourage them to work in pairs and to help each other.

Key

1 = flyover.
2 = intersection.
3 = junction.
4 = southbound.
5 = contraflow.

NB An intersection and a junction are similar. However, an intersection is normally larger and more complex than a junction.

Task 5
Listening

Tell the learners to look carefully at the three maps in their books. Ask if anyone recognises any of the places or has been to any of them.

Explain to the learners that they are going to hear the Traveline extract again and will have to identify the parts of the maps that are mentioned. It is important, therefore, that they are familiar with the routes marked. Spend a little time taking imaginary journeys with the class – describe a route and ask them to follow it on the map. E.g.: 'We are going from Reading to Maidenhead. We shall take the following route: we shall go on the M4 motorway . . . etc.'

Arrange the learners into pairs and tell them to listen and to identify those parts of the maps that are mentioned. Point out that information about other places is also given, but that they should ignore it.

Play the tape as many times as the learners feel necessary, pausing after each playing to allow them to discuss their answers. Finally, elicit their answers and check them with the tape.

Key

The parts of the maps mentioned are:
1 M4 nead Maidenhead, between junctions 9 and 10.

2 Piccadilly Circus and nearby streets.
3 A12 and M11 intersection at Redbridge.

Task 6
Listening and speaking

Arrange the learners into small groups and tell them that they are going to prepare their own Leisureline recording. This activity may be done in class or as a project at home. Learners will need to collect up-to-date information about leisure activities in their area from newspapers, entertainment guides, tourist office brochures, etc. If preferred, you could suggest they include only English-language entertainments, if that is possible in your area.

Explain that they will be making a short recording and that they should prepare it in writing first. Allow them to listen to the extract from the tape again so that they can use it as a model. If possible, ask the groups to record their message and then play all the messages to the rest of the class for them to comment on. If that is not possible, ask a spokesperson from each group to read their message to the class.

Task 7
Learner training

The aim of this task is to make the learners aware of opportunities for working on their English outside the classroom. Students often expect to learn only during the few hours a week that the class takes place, yet often there are many occasions in their everyday life when they could be learning too.

Tell the learners to work in small groups and to think about the occasions when they could use English on the telephone. Tell them first to look at the list in their books, as this will give them ideas. Then tell them to choose one of the occasions from their list and to make use of it in the next week, say. At the end of the week, ask the learners to report back to the class on what happened.